# ST. AUGUSTINE ACADEMY PRESS

## About Reverend P. Henry Matimore:

Patrick Henry Matimore was born in 1891 to Irish Immigrants in Chicago. After becoming a priest and receiving a doctorate in Sacred Theology, he briefly served as Superintendent of Schools for the Archdiocese of Chicago under Cardinal Mundelein from 1923-1926. By 1929, he was serving both as a professor of Education at Loyola University and as pastor of St. Clotilde's Church on the south side of Chicago. Despite his many duties, he still found time to produce a series of Catholic School Readers and to serve on the Advisory Board for the Journal of Religious Instruction. His parishioners affectionately remembered the good father strolling the neighborhood in the evenings with his dog "Rex," greeting all he met, especially the young people, for whom he always showed great concern. He retired in 1966, and died in 1972 at the age of 81.

## About *Heroes of God's Church:*

"This little book, which contains the lives of twenty-five saints told in dramatic narrative for chilren, is a distinct step in the right direction, since it makes the saints tangible, understandable objects for the hero worship of the young."

*—The Catholic Historical Review*, October 1933

This fifth grade volume in the Madonna Series is intended as a study in virtue using the stories of the Saints. Each one is presented, not merely as a two-dimensional figure for admiration, or a miracle worker, but as a real human in real-world situations, having to make tough decisions in order to become the *Heroes of God's Church.*

A CHILD'S GARDEN
OF
RELIGION STORIES

MATIM

**3**

WONDER
STORIES
OF
GOD'S PEOPLE

MATIMO

**4**

HEROES
OF
GOD'S CHURCH

MATIMORE

**5**

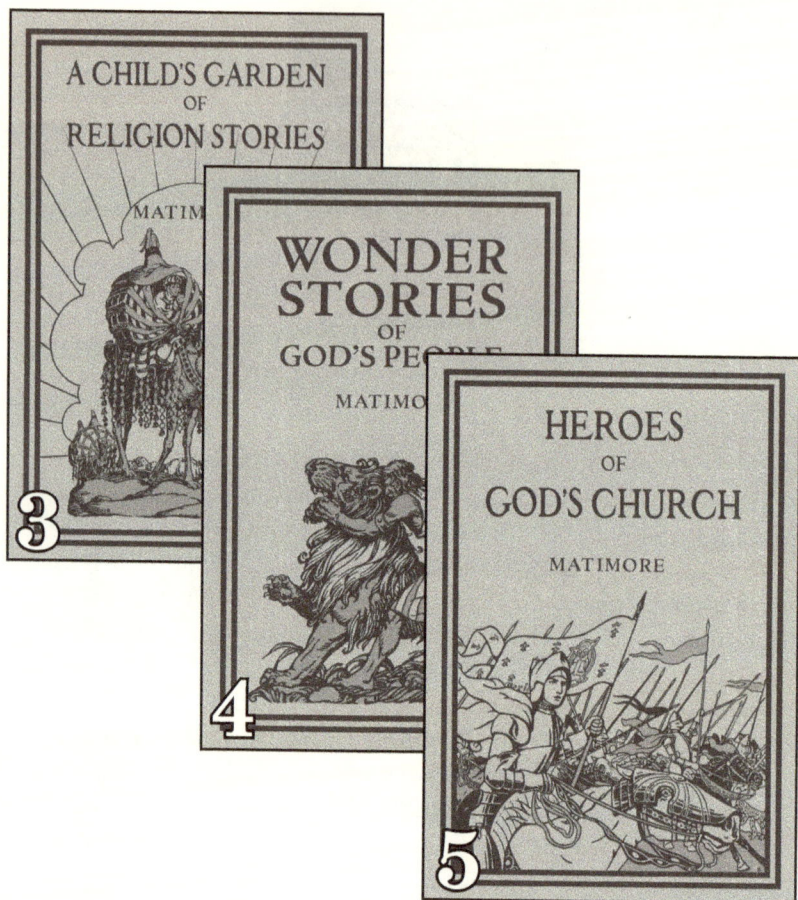

# THE MADONNA SERIES
by
## Rev. Patrick Henry Matimore
*Former Superintendent of Schools for the Archdiocese of Chicago*

This series of three study readers for the third through
fifth grade was originally produced in Chicago during the
reign of George Cardinal Mundelein in the early 1930s.
Each generously illustrated volume is based on stories from
the Bible and the Lives of the Saints.

THE MADONNA SERIES

A CHILD'S GARDEN OF RELIGION STORIES
WONDER STORIES OF GOD'S PEOPLE
HEROES OF GOD'S CHURCH

# HEROES OF GOD'S CHURCH

St. Louis and His Army Battling the Turks

# HEROES OF GOD'S CHURCH

By

## REVEREND P. HENRY MATIMORE, S.T.D.

FORMERLY SUPERINTENDENT OF SCHOOLS IN
THE ARCHDIOCESE OF CHICAGO

ILLUSTRATED BY

CARLE MICHEL BOOG

2018

ST. AUGUSTINE ACADEMY PRESS

HOMER GLEN, ILLINOIS

Nihil Obstat:

ARTHUR J. SCANLON, S.T.D.,
Censor Librorum.

Imprimatur:

✠ PATRICK CARDINAL HAYES,
Archbishop of New York.

April 24, 1931.

This book was originally published in 1931 by The Macmillan Company.
This facsimile edition reprinted in 2018 by St. Augustine Academy Press.

ISBN: 978-1-64051-073-9

To the
Sisters Teaching
in Our Schools

# FOREWORD

In writing the third volume of the Madonna Series, the purpose has been to acquaint our children with biographies that will have some particular influence on the development of their characters. Each story has been planned as a real character-training project, not merely as a reading lesson to inspire admiration for faith and religious heroism.

To accomplish this purpose, we have endeavored to stimulate interest in each saint by presenting him or her as a real human being who lived in a real world among real people and not as a superbeing surrounded by miraculous wonders. We have tried to make the saints human, admirable, and lovable, and therefore imitable. In order that children may learn that sanctity is not confined to any special nation or historical period, or time of life, or social or financial condition, saints have been chosen from various nations, from all periods of time, from all ages of life, and from all strata of society. Practically every type of sainthood is represented, from the martyr who shed his blood for Christ to the young Sister who did just the little things of life but did them well.

Each story is intended to bring out one or more situations in which the saint's virtue is emphasized. It is sincerely hoped that teachers will take advantage of these situations to develop similar virtues in those entrusted to their care.

# CONTENTS

# TO THE CHILDREN

Dear Boys and Girls:

Sometimes our boys and girls have strange ideas about the saints. They think that God made them so different from other people that it is quite difficult to imitate them. Many, too, have the idea that saints lived only in the early ages of the Church. They never imagine that saints were real people, living in a real world in every age and in every nation.

We have written these stories to give you a better and truer idea of the saints. They were real human beings who were once boys and girls like you, who enjoyed playing the games of their day just as much as you enjoy playing your games to-day. Some were rich, others poor. Some were of noble birth, others came from humble families. Some died young, others lived to old age. Some belonged to one nation, some to another. Some lived in the times of long ago, others lived in our own day. Some did great deeds in the service of God, others did the little things but did them well.

All this is to show you that saints do not belong to any special class of society or time in history. They are found in all states of life and in all ages of the world. A man can be a saint in almost any walk of life at any time.

Sanctity in our holy Church is not measured by wealth or position, by glory or power, but by a life well spent in the service of our God.

We hope these stories will help you to know and love the saints and inspire you to imitate them in their love and devotion for our divine Savior.

# HEROES OF GOD'S CHURCH

# SAINT CECILIA

*(Died 230)*

## 1. THE DAYS OF PERSECUTION

For almost three hundred years after the death of our Lord, the church suffered bitterly from persecutions on the part of the pagans. Things became so dreadful that it meant death to be a Christian. The powerful pagan government of Rome did all that it could to stamp out the first seeds of Christianity.

It became impossible for the followers of Christ to worship above ground. They dug long, narrow, secret passages, called *catacombs*, under the ground, where they held their sacred services. Before sunrise the Christians hurried cautiously through the winding streets and along the Appian Road to the catacombs of St. Callixtus. Here Mass was celebrated and Holy Communion given by the bishop or a priest helping him. Mass was usually followed by a short sermon and a few hymns. Before the people of Rome were roused from their slumbers, the faithful were hastening back to their homes in the city.

1

## 2. Cecilia Becomes Engaged

It was during these sad days of persecution that Cecilia lived. Hers was one of the great families of Rome, being both noble and wealthy. Cecilia's father was an honorable pagan, admired and respected by all who knew him. He never interfered with the faith of his wife, who was a devout Christian, and he even arranged to have his servants accompany St. Cecilia and her mother to the Christian meetings so that they would run no risk of being taken by the Roman soldiers.

Cecilia was the idol of his heart. With pride he watched her grow from babyhood and childhood to a charming young lady of seventeen. His friends had often remarked to him about the grace and beauty of his daughter, hinting that their sons would like to seek her hand in marriage. But the careful father turned them aside, one by one, till Valerian came.

Like Cecilia, Valerian was of noble birth and he owned vast estates. He was a virtuous pagan, some years older than Cecilia. The father of the charming maiden liked him and thought that he would be a most acceptable husband for his daughter. Valerian was delighted. He had succeeded where so many others had failed.

When Cecilia heard of her father's plans, her heart almost stopped beating. She had no intention of marrying any man, but she dared not offend her father, who seemed so happy in the choice. The poor girl made no answer to her father's proposal. Hurrying to her room, she burst into tears. She sobbed and sobbed as if her heart were broken.

After some time, Cecilia calmed herself and sought help in prayer. "O dear Lord," she said, "what shall I do? To please You and Your holy Mother, I have vowed to live a virgin all my life. If I tell this to my father, he will be angry and will become bitter against our holy faith. My vow I shall never break. Tell me, O Lord, what am I to do?"

The sweet voice of her guardian angel whispered: "Trust in God. All things will be done according to His divine will."

Relying on the help of God, St. Cecilia wiped away her tears. Lest her parents might see her flushed cheeks, she strolled through the gardens that surrounded the palace. No more tears were shed. There were no more pangs of sorrow.

## 3. THE WEDDING FEAST

The busy days just before the wedding were soon at hand. The proud father of Cecilia was determined that no Roman bride should surpass his daughter in glory on her wedding day. Money was spent lavishly. The palace was decorated with rich draperies scented with the choicest perfumes from Arabia. Flowers from the royal gardens were placed about the halls in golden vases. Delicious wines, fruits, vegetables, and meats were prepared.

The great day arrived. Guests in their silks and satins were met at the gates by torchbearers, and escorted to the palace. Dressed in flowing robes of cloth of gold and decked with precious jewels, Cecilia became the bride of Valerian.

African slaves moved silently about the banquet hall, carrying golden dishes with their tasty foods. Choice wines were freely poured into shining goblets. The hearty laughter of the Romans grew louder and louder as they drank to the health of the bride.

## 4. CECILIA TELLS HER SECRET

The parents of the bride were delighted. Valerian was the happiest man in the world. Cecilia, however, was nervous. She knew that she must tell her husband about her vow. She whispered a word at the table and she and her husband arose to make room for some of the other guests. Arm in arm, they walked across the gleaming marble floor and out into the garden.

Once in the garden they strolled among the rose bushes. Cecilia led the way to a bench where they could talk alone.

"Valerian," she began, "I have a secret to tell you, but swear to me that you will tell no one what I say."

Valerian, with a look of surprise, gazed into the beautiful face of his wife. He saw that she was very much in earnest. "I promise to tell no one," he said.

"I am a Christian," she said, "a loyal follower of the Savior Who died on Calvary for you and me. To Him, I have promised to be a virgin all the days of my life and He has sent an angel to guard and protect me. These many months, I have prayed for you, asking God to grant that you, too, might see the truth as I see it."

Valerian had never heard such things before. For a moment he did not know what to say. Then he spoke: "Where is this guardian angel that you speak about? Show him to me."

"O Valerian," she answered, "that holy spirit would never appear to pagan eyes." She saw that her husband was becoming interested. She told him how much her religion meant to her. She said that it had woven itself around every action in her life. "I would sooner die a thousand deaths than give it up," she cried.

"I should like to know more about this religion that you love so dearly. Perhaps I, too, could become a Christian," answered Valerian.

## 5. AT THE CATACOMBS

Cecilia was delighted. She explained to her husband that on that very night there would be a special meeting of the Christians at the catacombs on the Appian Way. She whispered to him the password and told him to hasten thither.

Without much difficulty, he found the secret place some miles beyond the gates of Rome. A Christian stood guard, ready to give the alarm of approaching danger. Valerian gave the password to the guard and was taken to Pope Urban. When the pope heard that the visitor came from Cecilia, he raised his eyes to heaven and, clasping his hands, murmured, "Thanks be to God."

That night God allowed a great miracle to take place. In a vision, Valerian saw St. Paul with an open book in his hand standing beside Pope Urban. "Read these words," said St. Paul, showing the book to Valerian.

The visitor read, "One Lord, one faith, one baptism, one God and father of all, who is above all, and through all and in us all."

"Do you believe?" asked the vision.

Cecilia's prayers were answered, for at that moment the grace of God entered the soul of Valerian, and he answered, "I believe."

The vision then disappeared.

With a lighted taper in his hand, Pope Urban led Valerian down the long flight of stairs carved in the hard clay. Then they walked through long, narrow, twisting passages that never saw the light of day. The sides of the walls were covered with white slabs of marble, enclosing niches in which were buried the bodies of Christians.

Valerian grew nervous as his companion kept walking on through the low, black corridors. The faint sound of music was heard. It grew louder and louder as they proceeded. At last they entered a large room far below the surface of the earth, with no windows and no lights, except the faint smoky flames from tiny oil lamps that were hung about the walls.

A priest in his sacred vestments was standing at the altar, giving a sermon to the faithful. Valerian paused to listen. The preacher warned the people that a new persecution was breaking out. He pleaded with them to remain faithful to Christ to the end, picturing for them an eternal happiness in God's kingdom. The simple, earnest words touched the soul of Valerian.

When the sermon was finished, Pope Urban beckoned Valerian to follow him into another smaller room. Here the earthen walls were covered with crude pictures of our Lord and the saints. These were painted on the plaster that had been placed on the rough walls. There was only one chair in the room and a plain, marble bench near the altar. Urban sat upon this and invited his companion to sit on the step of the altar.

## 6. Valerian Is Baptized

The kind old bishop stroked his long, gray beard as he explained the teachings of the church to Valerian. His voice was soft and low. There was something about him that inspired love and confidence in the pagan who sat at his feet. By the grace of God, the words of the bishop brought light to the Roman's mind. His soul was flooded with grace, and he fell on his knees before the successor of St. Peter and cried out, "I believe, O Urban, I believe."

The venerable pope bowed his head. Tears of joy trickled down his wrinkled cheeks and a fervent prayer fell from his trembling lips. God had granted the wish of St. Cecilia.

Valerian's heart was happy, both for his own sake and the sake of his lovely bride. He was led to the crude baptismal fount that one of the converts had carved from a white marble column. The angels of heaven rejoiced when the saving words of baptism were pronounced over him.

Urban embraced his new disciple with the affection of a father.

"My son," he said, "you are now a follower of Christ, the God-Man who died on Calvary for the souls of men. With a brave heart may you go forth from this sacred meeting place, determined to help others receive the priceless gift that you have received this morning. May the grace of God be with you and encourage you in the trying days that are to come."

The pope brought Valerian back to the large chapel that they had left some time before. The air was heavy with the smoke from the olive-oil lamps. Two wax candles in earthenware holders burned upon the stone table that served as an altar. The tinkling of the bell had just announced the consecration of the Mass. Fifty heads were bowed in silent adoration. For the first time in his life, Valerian knelt before the altar and adored Jesus, his God.

After Mass, Valerian was introduced to the other Christians. The men embraced him and the women gave a smile of welcome. They had all prayed for the conversion of the husband of their friend, Cecilia.

## 7. HOME AGAIN

It was just before sunrise when Valerian left the catacombs. He had spent the night with the faithful friends of Cecilia and promised to live and die with them. His anxiety to tell the good news to his wife hastened his steps. He was truly proud of his new-found faith, proud that he adored the same God as Cecilia.

As he entered the garden surrounding his home, everything was silent. A few hours before, that palace was aglow with lights and ringing with mirth and laughter. Now, not even a leaf on the tall oak trees was stirring.

The servants had left a few oil lamps burning dimly in the great reception room. Fearing to disturb the household, Valerian tiptoed through the hall to a richly decorated parlor. As he drew aside the heavy blue draperies, he saw his beautiful bride, still clad in her wedding dress, kneeling in prayer before a crucifix hanging on the wall. Her delicate, white hands were clasped upon her breast. Her eyes were raised toward heaven. How lovely, how pure, how good she looked that morning!

Valerian held his breath, lest he might startle his holy bride. He did not wish to intrude upon such a sacred scene, but to withdraw was impossible. Silent and still as a statue, Valerian waited for Cecilia to finish her prayers. She prayed aloud: "O sweet Jesus, from the bottom of my heart I thank Thee for the conversion of Valerian. He is one of us now. Together, night and day, we shall work for Thy holy cause."

## 8. The Mystery Clears

Valerian was dumbfounded. "How did she find out about my conversion?" he wondered. "Surely no messenger came before me to the house to tell her."

In his surprise, he forgot himself and coughed. Cecilia was startled. Her face turned pale. She jumped to her feet and turned to glance at the intruder.

When she saw Valerian, she threw herself into his arms and cried with joy: "Thank God, it is you. O Valerian, you can never imagine how happy I am to know that you are a Christian. Ever since you asked to marry me, I have prayed night and day for your conversion. Now we can face the whole world together and fight for the cause of Christ."

"But my beloved," asked Valerian, "how do you know that I am a Christian? Has someone been here before me with the good news?"

"As soon as you left," she answered, "I placed that crucifix on the wall and I have knelt before it in prayer ever since. Our dear Lord let me know how His grace and the kind words of the bishop were affecting your soul. At the moment of your baptism, my guardian angel appeared to me and told me the joyful news."

"What does your guardian angel look like?", asked Valerian. "I should be glad —" The sentence was never finished. A golden bright light shone in the room and in the midst of it appeared a beautiful angel in snow-white robes. A feeling of terror crept over Valerian, but Cecilia placed her arm in his and assured him that the sudden visitor was her guardian angel.

The angel spoke kindly to the happy couple. He placed sparkling golden crowns upon their heads to show that they both would be crowned martyrs in heaven. Turning to the surprised husband, the angel said: "God promises to grant anything that you wish for. Name your desire and it will be granted."

"God could grant me no greater favor," said Valerian, "than to give my twin brother the gift of faith."

A short time later Valerian stood beside the baptismal fount as the bishop poured the holy waters of baptism over Tiberius, his twin brother.

## 9. ZEALOUS APOSTLES

God's blessing rested on the home of Valerian and Cecilia. It was an earthly paradise, with the saintly wife as its queen and her husband as its king. The servants were treated with a kindness that had never been heard of before. Cecilia meekly went among them, teaching them about Jesus and His holy church. Sometimes the Christians gathered secretly in the house for the celebration of the Mass. On those occasions, the priest always preached to them a short sermon on Jesus, the miracle worker of Galilee.

THE GUARDIAN ANGEL CROWNS CECILIA AND VALERIAN

Valerian and Tiberius became zealous workers in the church. They gave money generously for the care of the poor, suffering Christians. Secret messages were sent to the Christians through them because they were never suspected of being followers of Christ. With little danger, therefore, they visited those who were imprisoned for their faith and gave them a word of cheer, urging them to remain loyal and true to the religion of Jesus Christ. Many a wavering soul was saved by their kind encouragement. At times these holy men, unknown to the guards, brought Holy Communion to those who were to be put to death for the faith.

Things had been going along quietly for several months and no eye of suspicion had been cast at the twin brothers. As they were men of wealth and prominence, the Roman soldiers always saluted them. All the prisons and courts were open to them, because they were looked upon as noble pagans wandering about to satisfy their curiosity.

## 10. CONDEMNED

But alas, some vile enemy betrayed them to the Roman police as being Christians. They were arrested and cast into the gloomy jails that they had visited so often. The greedy soldiers gloated over their rich prize. The officers were soon debating how they would divide the riches of their prisoners. All Rome gossiped about the sad plight of Valerian and Tiberius.

The brothers were hailed before a stern judge, who demanded that they offer sacrifice to the pagan gods. On their refusal they were beaten with lashes. Bruised and bleeding, they fearlessly defied the judge.

"Our heads will never bow before a god of bronze or stone," they cried. "Our God is a living God and Him alone do we adore."

Shouts of "Death! Death!" rose from the rabble that attended the trial. The judge bowed his approval and the prisoners were led off to death. They had known Christ but a short time and now they were to suffer death for Him and receive His crown of glory.

The prefect of Rome and his friends rejoiced in the approaching death of these two wealthy Christians. They made hurried plans for the division of the brothers' riches among themselves. But Valerian and his brother, knowing that their death was certain, gave their palace to Cecilia and the rest of their wealth to Christian friends to be used for the poor. When the prefect found this out, he was enraged. His plans had come to nothing.

## 11. CECILIA JOINS THE MARTYRS

But these bloodthirsty men were not finished with their wicked work. They decided to arrest Cecilia as a Christian and to take whatever she owned. Forcing their way into her home, they dragged her out and cast her in a filthy prison as if she were a criminal.

Everyone who knew the charming Christian widow loved her. The prefect was, therefore, timid about condemning her to death. In various ways he tried to coax her to give up her faith and turn to the pagan gods of Rome.

"Cecilia will never offer sacrifice to false gods," she exclaimed. "I have pledged my soul to the great God Who, in the days of old, walked the earth with Abraham, Isaac, and Jacob. Throughout my life I have served His divine Son Who died on Calvary's cross for the love of you and me. Shall I fall down and adore a piece of marble? Shall I burn incense before an image of stone? Never! No, never!"

"But remember," said the judge, "unless you do as I ask, I shall be forced to condemn you to suffering and, perhaps —"

Cecilia did not give him a chance to finish. "There is no punishment in your power that can make me deny the Lord Jesus Christ," she said. "I have loved and served Him till now and I shall continue to do so till death. Let the law take its course. The Christian asks for no mercy."

If Cecilia had had any chance of escaping death before, she had none after this speech. The judge con-

demned her to be steamed to death in her own home.
The brave girl was hurried to her palace during the
night and locked in a room used for steam baths. All
night scalding steam was poured into this room, but it
had no effect on Cecilia.

The judge was both surprised and angry when he
found that his prisoner still lived. He sent one of the
soldiers to the house to behead her. Only three blows
of the sword were allowed by the Roman law. The
blows fell upon the neck of the condemned girl but
they did not cut the head from the body. The
soldier placed his bloody sword in its scabbard and
returned to report to the prefect.

For several days the saint lay dying. Drop by drop,
she was shedding her blood for the sake of Jesus Christ.
The Christians came to visit her and to receive a smile
or a word of encouragement to keep up the good fight.
She gave all her wealth to the poor, suffering Christians
of Rome, begging God to bless them and help them.

Slowly her strength gave out with the loss of blood.
"How sweet it is to die for the Lord," she whispered
faintly and closed her eyes in death.

The body of St. Cecilia was buried in the catacombs.
Several hundred years later, the grave was opened and
the body was found to be just as beautiful as when it
was first buried. It was then placed in a marble tomb
in the church of St. Cecilia.

TRUE OR FALSE

Number a paper from 1 to 12.   After each number write $T$ if the statement to which it corresponds is true;  write $F$ if the statement is false.

1. The early Christians had beautiful churches.
2. The catacombs were built underground.
3. Cecilia's father was a pagan.
4. Cecilia had a fine wedding.
5. Valerian was not surprised when he heard Cecilia's secret.
6. Valerian saw Pope Urban holding a book.
7. Pope Urban led the way with a lamp.
8. On the night of her wedding, Cecilia told Valerian her secret.
9. Valerian was proud of his faith.
10. An angel told Cecilia about the conversion of Valerian.
11. Cecilia treated her servants harshly.
12. She was steamed to death.

# SAINT SEBASTIAN

*(Died 288)*

## 1. THE ARRIVAL OF THE EMPEROR

"Make way! Make way! The emperor passes!",
shouted two black slaves, as they hurried through the
narrow streets of Rome, clearing the way for the Roman
ruler.

Passers-by withdrew to the sides of the streets or
into archways to watch the solemn procession pass. A
red-faced tyrant sat alone in a gorgeous jeweled chariot
drawn by four powerful, African slaves. Behind him
on horseback followed the favorite captains in the
emperor's army. Sebastian was among them, a handsome, finely built soldier not more than twenty-five
years of age. There was something noble about his
bearing that made people notice him.

The emperor turned neither to the right nor to the
left as his subjects bowed before him and cheered him
with their lusty cries of "Long live Maximilian, our
divine ruler!" At last the slave-horses stopped before
the entrance to one of the great courts of the city. All
day long the court had been the scene of excitement.

It was the day appointed for hearing the cases of those who had been arrested as Christians.

Throughout the afternoon, singly and in small groups the poor Christians had appeared before the heartless prefect of Rome to answer to the charge of being believers in Christ. To be found guilty of the charge in those days meant death.

The judge tried to coax and persuade some to give up their religion. Others he tried to force. But the result was always the same. The Christians to a man were loyal to the faith of Jesus Christ. The prefect was angry and tired after his fruitless efforts. Sharply he ordered the prisoners back to the filthy dungeons to give them time to change their minds.

The bronze doors of the palace were swung open for the emperor just as the last prisoners left the court-room. The wicked ruler was anxious to get a report of the work of the day. He sat upon a marble throne at one end of the room, with his captains in gay uniforms standing to the right and the left.

The prefect of Rome and his helpers made their reports. They told of the refusal of the Christians to offer sacrifice to the gods of Rome. The emperor gnashed his teeth and swore that he would teach the Christians a lesson that they would never forget.

"I shall wipe the memory of their God from the face of the earth," he said. "I shall make the death of every Christian so painful that no man will dare join their ranks. 'Death to every Christian man, woman, and child in the land' will be our watchword."

## 2. THE BETRAYAL

"Most gracious emperor," said one of the captains who stepped from the left of the throne, "it is my duty to inform you that among the chosen friends of your household, there stands a traitor to you and the gods of Rome."

"Be careful, my captain," answered Maximilian angrily. "Those of our household have been chosen because of their loyalty to our empire and their devotion to our person. Let him beware who dares speak ill of them in our presence."

"But most kind emperor, I beg thee hear me to the end," pleaded the informer.

"Be quick then, sir, and, by all the gods of Rome, if you accuse wrongly, I shall cast you to the wild beasts in the arena," threatened the emperor.

"I shall have no difficulty in proving all that I have to say," answered the captain. "Be it known to you, then, that among the captains of your cohorts, there is one who has sworn loyalty to the Christian God, one who goes about the prisons and encourages the Christians to remain faithful to their religion."

"Enough, false friend! Prove what you say or I

SEBASTIAN ADMITS HE IS A CHRISTIAN

shall run this sword through your heart," cried the furious ruler, lunging forward with his jeweled sword in hand.

"Stay your hand, most gracious emperor," said Captain Sebastian, as he bravely stepped before the throne. "There is no need of proof. I am a Christian, a loyal, devoted follower of Jesus Christ but none the less a loyal, devoted subject of the emperor of Rome."

### 3. A FEARLESS SOLDIER OF CHRIST

Maximilian was dazed. The sword fell from his hand. Was he dreaming? Had he heard aright? Sebastian, his beloved Sebastian, a Christian! Sebastian, the bravest and truest of his captains! "Impossible!" he murmured. "It cannot be true."

When the emperor recovered from his shock of surprise, he gazed at the stalwart soldier who stood before him. "But, Sebastian," he pleaded, "there is some mistake."

"No, there is no mistake," answered the brave captain. "Long before you honored me, I had become a follower of Christ."

"But my friend, one day you will lead the armies of Rome on foreign battlefields and you will return crowned as the great hero of Rome. Don't you understand, Sebastian?" pleaded Maximilian again. "Offer sacrifice to the gods of Rome and let us forget all about this God of the Christians."

"Noble emperor," said Sebastian, "in the years that are past, you have favored me with kindness and with honors. For them I am grateful from the bottom of my heart. For you and my beloved country I would gladly lay down my life, — yes, gladly shed every drop of my blood in their defense. But to the false gods of Rome, I cannot offer sacrifice. Sebastian, the Christian, can never bow the knee before idols, before statues of stone and bronze that have no life. The God whom I adore is the great, living God Who made the earth, the moon, the stars, the sun, Who made you and me, and before Whom one day we shall all stand to be judged. To that God alone shall I offer sacrifice. Him alone shall I adore."

It grieved the emperor deeply to think that his trusted friend was a follower of Christ. He saw that it was useless to argue further. His love turned to hate and his wrath now broke forth upon the captain of the cohorts.

"Very well, ungrateful wretch," he cried. "I shall teach you and your friends a lesson that you will never forget. You have proved a traitor to the trust I placed in you. You spurned the generous offers I made to you. All for the sake of the God of the Christians. For your crime, I condemn you to suffer a long-drawn-out death that will satisfy me for the grief you have caused me."

Then turning to the captain of the archers, he commanded: "At the break of dawn, take this traitor to yonder royal gardens. Bind him hand and foot. Then let your skilled archers shoot him with arrows. See that the darts do not kill him quickly, but fill that proud body with arrows till it bleeds to death."

### 4. THE SENTENCE IS FULFILLED

The heart of the captain of the archers sank when he received the order. He had often met Sebastian and admired his noble, generous character. But the emperor's command was law and had to be obeyed.

The sun had scarcely risen the following morning, when Sebastian was stripped of his military uniform and bound to an olive tree. Some of the archers hated the Christians and therefore took a special delight in carrying out the emperor's decree. Arrow after arrow whizzed through the air and pierced the flesh of the prisoner. Soon tiny streams of blood were trickling from the wounds. In their brutality, the archers waited between attacks and laughed at the agony of their victim.

When they had finished their task, the body of Sebastian, covered with blood, fell over. The cords around the waist held it to the tree. Thinking him dead, the soldiers cut these cords and let the body fall to the ground.

## 5. The Return to Life

The news of Sebastian's death soon reached the Christians. Irene, a faithful Christian widow, hurried to the garden with several servants to bury the body of the martyr. Imagine her surprise when she saw the blood-covered breast rise and fall as Sebastian breathed!

The servants carried their precious burden to her home. A Christian doctor examined the saint's body and saw that the arrows had made only skin wounds. He assured the happy woman that, with good care, her patient could soon take up his work again for the friends of Christ.

The home of Irene became a sort of sanctuary for the Christians. They were glad to gather there and listen to the advice of Sebastian, who by this time was almost well. When the wounds had finally healed, Sebastian was warned to leave Rome for some safer place, but no urging could induce him to desert his Christian friends.

"Sebastian is no coward," he said. "I shall live and die in Rome, fighting the cause of God and His people."

## 6. Before the Emperor Again

One day Sebastian heard that Maximilian was going to pass through a certain passageway in the palace.

The saint stationed himself at the head of the stairs and waited the arrival of the emperor. Maximilian was panting as he neared the top of the long flight of stairs and paused for breath.

He was startled by a voice calling his name, "Maximilian, Maximilian!" Was it a voice from the grave? He recognized it at once. His red face turned pale. His limbs began to quiver. He looked above and saw Sebastian. The emperor stood motionless.

"Maximilian," said Sebastian, "the blood of thousands of Christians that you have put to death cries to heaven for vengeance. Turn your sword away from the followers of Christ. Give up your sinful ways and fight under the banner of the one and only living and true God."

When the emperor realized that it was Sebastian in his flesh and blood that was talking to him, he was overcome with rage.

"This time, ungrateful traitor," he thundered, "I shall be sure of your death." Then calling the guards, he commanded them to put Sebastian to death while he watched them.

A smile of satisfaction covered his face when he saw that the deed was completed. He kicked the lifeless form of his former favorite as only a cruel person would kick a dog.

"Throw the body into the large sewer," he ordered,

"so that none of his friends will be able to give him an honorable burial."

Under cover of night the soldiers hurled the body of Sebastian into the filthy sewer. But that very night the saint appeared to another Christian, telling her where his body was and asking her to have it buried with those of the other Christians.

Next day in the catacombs was buried the body of one of God's heroes, St. Sebastian.

### Something to Find

Find the sentence or sentences that prove the following statements are correct or incorrect.

1. Two horses drew the emperor's chariot.
2. The emperor waved to the people.
3. The prefect was kind to his prisoners.
4. The emperor loved Sebastian.
5. The emperor tried to save Sebastian.
6. The emperor hated Sebastian when he found that he was a Christian.
7. Maximilian ordered a quick death for Sebastian.
8. Sebastian was shot by the archers in the morning.
9. A pagan doctor said that Sebastian would get well.
10. Maximilian was afraid when he heard the voice of Sebastian.

# SAINT AGNES

(291-304)

## 1. ROME'S TRIBUTE

It is the twenty-first of January, the feast of St. Agnes. Light clouds, tinged with pink, float across the eastern sky but the early morning air is sharp and chilly. A steady stream of people is passing through the gates of Rome on their way to the church of St. Agnes. In groups of two and three they hurry along, anxious to be on time for the early Mass.

The famous, old church is gorgeously decorated in honor of the occasion. Lighted candles without number have been placed about the church in crystal chandeliers. The tiny, yellow flames which continually dance and flicker reflect themselves in the sparkling crystals. Scarlet and gold draperies of silk and damask cover the massive marble pillars from ceiling to floor, and reach from arch to arch in graceful folds. Flowers and palms surround the marble altar which contains the beautiful shrine of St. Agnes.

Soon the church is filled with people. Nuns and priests join with the faithful in honoring this heroine

of God's church.   From one of the balconies, the joyful peals of the organ announce that the bishop is
about to begin Mass.   Boys' voices, sweet and clear
like those of angels, blending with the deep basses of
the men, thrill the hearts of the people.

## 2. THE LAMBS OF ST. AGNES

The Mass is now over.   The choir breaks forth in a
beautiful hymn in honor of St. Agnes.   The people
make way as a procession of altar boys, dressed in
white cassocks with red sashes and carrying lighted
torches, wends its way from the rear of the church
toward the altar.   All eyes are turned to the two little
boys at the end of the line.   Between them they carry
a basket covered with white silk, in which lie two tiny,
snow-white lambs with silk ribbons tied around their
necks.   These are the spotless lambs of St. Agnes.

Each year on her feast day, two pure, little lambs
are placed on her altar and blessed.   They are then
given to the care of Sisters, who save their wool and
make it into *palliums*.   These are the long, narrow
white cloths that are worn by archbishops over the
shoulders to show that the archbishop is the good
shepherd who rules his priests and people.

The little, innocent, white lambs are signs of holiness
and purity.   Very often we see pictures of St. Agnes
holding a lamb in her arms; the lamb is to remind us

of how gentle and pure she was. Indeed she is a wonderful model for all boys and girls.

### 3. AGNES REJECTS HER ADMIRERS

Agnes was a beautiful girl, born in a rich and noble Roman family. She was so lovely and so kind that all the wealthy, young noblemen of Rome admired and loved her. Even though she was but a child of thirteen, many thought of marrying her. This was not strange because, in those days, people married when quite young. So, one by one, these young men told the sweet and gentle Agnes of their love. But St. Agnes, in her own charming manner, sent them away with the answer that she would give her heart to no earthly lover because the One Whom she loved dwelt far beyond the skies.

Most of the young men were honorable and respected Agnes' wishes. There was one, however, who was determined to marry her whether she consented or not. This was Fluvius, the son of Sympronius, the prefect or governor of Rome. He made up his mind to force the holy Agnes to become his wife.

Time and again, he called at her home, only to be sent away by the servants. Often he hid himself in the beautiful gardens that surrounded her palace and as Agnes wandered with her maids among the flowers and shrubs, he would approach her. But each time, when Agnes saw him, she hastened toward the house or dismissed him with a cold greeting. This only enraged the evil man all the more.

## 4. AGNES IN HER GARDEN

One evening he waited again for Agnes in the garden. He was determined this night to force the saintly maiden to consent to marry him. Happy and lovely in her rich, white dress and her beautiful cloak, she walked in and out among the flower beds, pausing here and there to gather the choicest and sweetest flowers. As she plucked the blossoms, she passed them to her maids that they, too, might enjoy their delicious perfume. The son of the governor was hiding behind the tall bushes. The object of his love never looked more charming than she did now as she stood among her flowers in the soft moonlight. She seemed to him like a silver goddess. By fair means or foul, he would have her as his bride.

Silently and cautiously, he stepped through the grass until he drew near a marble bench toward which St. Agnes was walking. To Fluvius, it seemed that she would never arrive at the seat. She and her maids drew nearer and nearer. At last, she arrived at the bench and, as she seated herself, Fluvius heard her say to her maids, "I shall rest here a while and enjoy the cool, perfumed air." The maids bowed and stood a few steps away.

## 5. The Revenge of Fluvius

St. Agnes had no sooner sat down than Fluvius stepped from the bushes and stood before her. She was startled, and a low cry of terror escaped from her lips. Fluvius assured her that he meant no harm and threw himself upon his knees at her feet. He poured forth words of love, telling the frightened girl that he would die if she sent him away again.

The feelings of St. Agnes toward Fluvius were of disgust mingled with pity. His sinful life displeased her and she knew that he was more in love with her wealth than with her beauty but she felt sorry for him as he knelt there.

She rose from the bench. "Go," she commanded in a clear, firm voice, "go from my presence forever. I shall never marry you nor any other man. I have already pledged myself to my heavenly Spouse."

This answer was too much for the proud son of the Roman prefect. He jumped from his knees. With anger in his voice and shaking his finger in the calm face of Agnes, he cried out: "Very well, then, young maiden! I shall denounce you to-morrow as a Christian. You know what that means."

The child knew only too well what it meant — a painful and horrible death. But she smiled in the face of her heartless betrayer and pointed toward the gate. The rejected suitor pulled his cloak about him and disappeared into the night.

## 6. Agnes Arrested

Early the next morning, all Rome was startled with the news that the charming Agnes had been arrested as a Christian. She was to be tried immediately and her judge was to be Sympronius, the father of Fluvius.

Sympronius was anxious that his son should marry this wealthy, noble maiden. When she was brought before him, he spoke to her kindly at first. He tried to coax her to agree to the marriage, picturing for her a happy and brilliant life as the wife of the son of the prefect of Rome. But his pleading and coaxing did not influence Agnes. She remained firm and calm.

Finally, Sympronius lost his patience and began to threaten his prisoner with all sorts of punishments. But the prisoner smiled sweetly at him and let him know that she had no fear of him or his punishments. Thus enraged, the judge ordered Agnes to be handcuffed and cast into prison. There, he thought, she would soon change her mind. The soldiers tried to fasten handcuffs on the wrists of St. Agnes but the smallest were too large for her little, white arms. Her hands were then tied with cords and bound behind her back, and like a criminal she was led to jail.

## 7. BEFORE THE CRUEL JUDGE

The next day, the prisoner was again brought before her judge. This time, she was commanded to accept the proposal of marriage. Again she spurned the offer.

The judge leaned forward and muttered through his teeth, "Young maiden, do you not know that I have the power of life and death over you? You are a Christian."

But Agnes was not frightened. She turned her lovely blue eyes toward him and said, "Yes, I am a Christian and to Christ alone am I pledged."

Fire was now burning in the eyes of the judge. He could not stand to have this mere child defy him. "Since you are so anxious to remain unmarried," he said, "I shall send you to live with the vestal virgins and in company with them you shall serve the gods of Rome."

"O noble judge," she exclaimed, "do you think that I who serve the living God would adore your pagan idols — gods that are deaf and dumb, gods that are made of bronze and stone? Agnes will never bend her knee before the gods of Rome. Agnes, the Christian, fears them not."

This daring answer was an insult to the governor of Rome. He thought for a moment. Then he decided on a scheme that he felt sure would bring this stubborn girl to terms. He knew that as a Christian, Agnes prized her purity more dearly than life. "Then I shall send you to a place," he said, "where you will soon lose that virtue that you so highly prize."

The innocent girl was shocked for a moment. Then, gazing at her cruel judge, she said: "I laugh at your threats. If you only knew who my God is, you would not dare to speak thus. An angel of the Lord is my guardian and the Son of God Himself will protect me."

God rewarded Agnes for her strong faith. In a wonderful manner, He guarded and protected her so that no harm came to her.

## 8. THE ROMAN RABBLE

Stories of the power of the God Whom Agnes loved, quickly passed through the city. The pagan priests feared the effect of these stories on the people, so they denounced Agnes as a witch and urged the people to clamor for her death. A howling mob gathered before the prison where Agnes had been put in a filthy dungeon. "Death to the Christian!" they cried. "Away with the witch! Death to the enemy of the gods of Rome!"

Imagine how the gentle little girl felt when she heard the Roman rabble demand her death! Poor, innocent child! Never had she harmed or injured anyone, and often she had delighted to give alms and food to the very ones who were now denouncing her. For a moment her heart was sad and tears filled her eyes. But when she remembered that she was to die for her God, she wiped away the tears and resolved to be calm and firm to the end.

## 9. AGNES IS CONDEMNED TO DEATH

The little saint was once more led before her judge. Sympronius was delighted at the cries of the mob. His smile encouraged them and louder and wilder went forth their demands that Agnes be put to death. The judge looked at the delicate child before him — a mere girl of thirteen years. No pity, no sympathy entered that stony heart.

"I beseech you not to consider my youth," Agnes said. "I seek no pity on that account. The God that I love and adore looks rather at the heart than at the age. I fear not your anger nor your punishments."

Never had a mere child roused the judge to such anger and hatred. "Silence, Christian witch!" he thundered. "I sentence you to be burned to death in the public square." The mob cheered and howled their approval.

The condemned girl gave the judge a smile of thanks. She clasped her little, white hands together, raised her eyes to heaven and prayed, "O Lord, I thank Thee for this great honor — the honor of dying for love of Thee."

## 10. FLAMES THAT DID NOT BURN

St. Agnes was soon placed upon a pile of wood. The wood had been covered with oil and pitch in order that it might burn more readily. Brutal soldiers fought for the honor of applying the torch to the wood. The flames spread rapidly, fanned by a gentle breeze. In a wild fury of delight, the mob yelled and cheered.

Higher and higher leaped the flames, casting their crimson glow upon the face of the saint who stood meekly in their midst. Eagerly the people watched her face for signs of pain, but they saw nothing but a heavenly smile. More wood was thrown upon the fire. Like the tongues of giant serpents, the flames flashed about the virgin in white, but no flame ever touched her nor did the fierce fire burn her.

The people were amazed. They beheld Agnes extend her hands and raise her eyes to heaven. They were silent for a moment, thinking that she was asking for mercy from her judge. But no, hers was a prayer of love to the great God Who rules on high.

"O Almighty God," she prayed, "ever to be loved and adored, I thank Thee because, through Thy divine Son, I have escaped from sinful men. I thank Thee,

CARLE MICHEL BOOG

SAINT AGNES IN THE FLAMES

O heavenly Father, Who makes me fearless even in the midst of flames and fills me with a desire to go to Thee. O God, I go to Thee in Whom I have believed and hoped, to Thee Whom I have loved so dearly."

As she finished her prayer, the flames fluttered and disappeared. There on the blackened mass of wood stood Agnes, unstained and untouched, in her robes of white.

But this miracle did not soften the hearts of her enemies. Cries for her death grew louder and fiercer. "Death to the witch! Death to the friend of the Christian God! Death to the enemy of Rome!"

## 11. DEATH BY THE SWORD

The judge then ordered one of the soldiers to behead the prisoner. With drawn sword, the soldier stepped forward. Agnes was led to the block. She fell upon her knees and whispered the dying prayer of her Master, "Father, into Thy hands I commend my spirit."

Then she placed her head upon the block. The sword fell and the soul of St. Agnes entered into the joyful company of martyrs and virgins who adore before the throne of God in heaven.

The mob was satisfied. The life of a gentle, holy girl had been sacrificed to satisfy their wicked hate and revenge. They hurried from the place, wondering when the blood of their next victim would be shed.

Soon there was no one near the scene of death but a few faithful Christians. They wrapped the body in linens and carried it to the home of Agnes' parents. Here it was prepared for burial.

In the darkness of the night, the Christians gathered to place the body of their friend in the catacombs. These were long, narrow, winding passages under the earth where the early Christians held their services and where they buried their dead.

With lighted torches in their hands, the faithful friends passed through twisting corridors, singing psalms and hymns. The procession halted in a little room where an altar had been placed. Two of the men dug a niche in the side of the wall, just large enough to hold the body of St. Agnes. The body was placed in the niche and a marble slab was sealed over it with the words, ST. AGNES, VIRGIN AND MARTYR.

### HELPS TO STUDY

1. Can you give a better title to this story?
2. Describe the Roman celebration for St. Agnes' feast day.
3. Of what are the white lambs a sign?
4. Why was Fluvius so anxious to marry Agnes?
5. What do you think of him?
6. How did the pagan priests turn the people against Agnes?
7. Tell what took place when St. Agnes stood before her judge.
8. Why did the fire not burn the saint?
9. Read the prayer of St. Agnes as she stood in the flames.
10. Describe her funeral.

# SAINT MONICA

*(332–387)*

## 1. Patricius

It was a gala day in Carthage when Monica married the wealthy Patricius, but there was little reason for anyone to be envious of the gentle Christian bride. Her husband was a fiery-tempered pagan who had little respect for the teachings of her faith.

At first the young bride trembled whenever the face of Patricius flushed with anger or when his gruff voice thundered out some command. But, timid as she was, Monica always gathered enough courage to argue with him or correct him. This increased his rage and caused him to heap more abuse upon her.

What should she do? His violent temper and his sharp tongue often brought sorrow to her heart. She had learned that it was useless to argue with him or thwart him in his fits of anger. She thought of the meek and gentle Master Who overcame the world by His meekness and resolved to imitate Him. Therefore when Patricius stalked about the house during his violent outbursts of temper, Monica remained meek and quiet as if she deserved whatever was said.

42

However, she always managed to straighten things out later in the day when Patricius was calm. Often in the evening she would lead him to some favorite nook in their garden to enjoy the cool sea breezes and listen to the laughter of their two boys as they raced over the gravel paths and through the berry bushes. St. Monica would wait her chance and then speak to Patricius about his fit of anger. She would gently show him how wrong and unjust he had been.

Casting his eyes on the ground or gazing steadily into the rippling fountain, he would listen patiently to St. Monica. Her tenderness would conquer him and he would plead for forgiveness. Time after time he promised, as they sat beneath the tall palm trees, to control his anger. He improved with the years but never became as patient and meek as his gentle and holy wife.

## 2. The Stubborn Son

Imagine how grieved and worried St. Monica was when she noticed that Augustine, her younger son, was becoming more and more like his father. On several occasions he had shown a stubborn, angry temper. Monica had trained her boys well because she wished them to be good Christians. With all her holy zeal, she was preparing them for the great day when they should be baptized and enrolled among the followers of

Christ. Full well she knew the dangers that beset them with pagan playmates and pagan teachers. Time and again, she warned them against the false teachings of their pagan friends. The loving mother felt that she had done her work well and had little to fear for the future of her boys.

What a blow she received when she heard that Augustine had joined the ranks of the anti-Christians! Could it be possible that the boy she brought up so carefully would turn his back on the God she loved and served? It was too terrible to be true. "It cannot be," she cried. "Have all my efforts been of no avail?"

Sad to say, it was only too true. Augustine, a bright, clever lad of seventeen years, had joined those who despised the God Whom Monica loved. She heard it from his own lips when he returned from school. Her loving heart was crushed when he told her that he knew too much to be a Christian and to believe their foolish teachings.

St. Monica was heartbroken. She withdrew to her room and shed tears of sorrow and anger. Her boy — her son — had become a traitor to her God. "It would have been better if he had never been born," she moaned as she paced the floor, wringing her hands. She tried to pray but could not; the shock was too great.

### 3. Banished from Home

The chirp of a bird drew her attention to the open window that faced the sea. She paused before it and gazed at the foamy waves as they dashed themselves upon the sandy shore. Fond memories of other days rose before her — memories of her boys playing on the sand or battling in the waves, as she prayed for them. How proud she had been as they grew into stalwart youths! But that pride was crushed now.

"For seventeen years," she sighed, "I have watched him and prayed for him. Morning, noon, and night, I have asked God to keep him good and holy and to protect him from evil. I had often dreamed of having him with me in heaven, but now — all is changed. He spurns the true God. He gives himself to sin and his soul to hell." The distracted woman cast herself upon a marble bench and wept bitterly. She arose shortly and brushed aside her tears. She had formed a plan to conquer the stubborn will of Augustine. Banishing him from home would bring him to his senses, she thought.

The echo of her son's voice reached her ears as he called to one of the servants in the garden. She resolved to make a last plea and if this failed, she would send the boy away from his home.

Followed by her faithful brown dog, she approached

the bench where Augustine was studying. The boy
was surprised to see the sad face of his mother. Kissing him, Monica begged him to give up his new friends
and return to the God he had spurned. He told her
very firmly that he had studied the matter most carefully and was convinced that she was in the wrong
and he was right. He was only a boy of seventeen, but
he felt that he was much wiser than his mother. A
mother's tears and a mother's pleadings had had no
effect on Augustine. There was nothing left for her to
do but carry out her determination.

"Augustine," she said, "there is no room in my
home for a traitor to my God. Ungrateful, stubborn
son, be gone from my presence forever!"

Augustine was dazed. Never before had he heard
his mother speak like this. Nervously pushing the
pebbles with his foot, he thought for a moment. He
was making his choice between his mother and his
friends. Too stubborn to give in, he decided in favor
of his friends and hastened to the house to gather up
some clothing and a few books. He left without a
word of farewell.

A mother's love had banished Augustine from his
home in order to bring him to his senses. Night and
day, St. Monica prayed for him. She pleaded with
God to have mercy on her wayward son and to bring
him back to see the truth. She asked the priests and

the bishop to reason with the boy. But the stubborn youth refused to listen to reason. The priests grew tired talking to him and they avoided his mother because the same cry was always on her lips, "Will you see my boy? Will you talk to Augustine? Will you pray for him?"

One day the good bishop, who was weary of listening to her pleadings, told her that he would trouble himself no more with the stubborn boy. This answer grieved the poor, distracted mother. She had determined to save her boy's soul and she would have no rest while that soul was in danger of damnation. Tears filled her eyes as she looked into the face of the bishop.

"Oh, good bishop," she cried, "during all these years have I prayed for him; during all these years have I wept for him. Yes, and gladly would I lay down my life for him. Do not tell me that there is no hope."

This tender plea was too much for the bishop. Blessing the weeping mother, he said: "My friend, continue your prayers. It is impossible that the child of such tears should be lost."

## 4. AUGUSTINE GOES TO ITALY

By this time, Monica had permitted Augustine to return home. Year followed year, but there was no change for the better in him. Finally when he was about twenty-nine years old, he decided to go to Rome to teach. Monica feared that life away from his native city would only delay his conversion and, perhaps, bring him in contact with still more evil companions. She used all her powers to induce him to remain at Carthage. But the call of Rome was ringing in his ears. His love for learning and adventure was stronger than his love for his mother.

Unknown to her, he boarded a small sailboat that had been lying at anchor in the harbor and sailed for Italy. When poor Monica heard the sad news, she hastened to the shore to bring her wayward boy home, but, alas! it was too late. The boat was fast disappearing from view.

"My boy is gone," she cried, "but I shall follow him. I have prayed and suffered too long to give up the struggle now."

St. Monica sailed on the next boat. She wished to be near her son to protect him as much as possible. Augustine's surprise was very great when his mother greeted him one day on the streets of Rome. Augustine and his mother lived for some time in Rome but Augustine was not contented. Milan, the city of the north, attracted him. Thither he went, accompanied by his mother and brother and a few friends. Monica was secretly pleased at this journey because the great St. Ambrose lived at Milan. Stories of his wonderful powers had long before reached the shores of Africa. New hope now dawned in Monica's heart.

"If Augustine would only meet Ambrose," she repeated over and over again.

One day, through curiosity, Augustine and some of his friends wandered into the church to hear St. Ambrose preach. They wondered if the stories about his wonderful sermons were true. The stirring sermon more than proved Ambrose's greatness. The curious visitors returned again and again. They listened to Ambrose as he denounced their sins and their errors.

## 5. CONQUERED

The grace of God began to work in Augustine. He made private visits to St. Ambrose, who clearly showed him the error of his ways. St. Monica was overjoyed when she heard this. However, she did not stop her prayers on the eve of victory; she doubled them. The great day finally came when Augustine was baptized and received into the church of God. The grace of God had brought success after thirteen years of prayers and tears, and the mother's prayer was answered.

Monica was satisfied and happy. She felt that her life work was over. She yearned for her home in far-away Carthage. Augustine was now more obedient to her wishes. He made arrangements for the home-ward journey. It was, indeed, a joyful group that set

THE BAPTISM OF SAINT AUGUSTINE

out from Milan — Monica, her two sons, and some of their friends. They traveled by land to Ostia, a seaport near Rome.

Here a deadly fever attacked St. Monica. She knew that her end was near. As Augustine sat at her bedside one day, she said to him, "My son, there is now nothing in life that gives me any pleasure. All my hopes in this world are now at an end. The only thing for which I desired to live was that I might see you a Christian and a child of heaven. I ask for nothing more. Be loyal and true to your God till death calls you."

During the next few days the fever increased and, in her delirium, Monica spoke of nothing else but her love and prayers for Augustine. He had never realized until now the terrible sorrow that he had brought into his mother's life. He stooped to kiss her fevered brow and his silent tears fell upon the holy face that had shed so many tears for him.

Just before the end, the dying mother opened her eyes and smiled at her sons. They told her that it grieved them to have her die in a strange land, far removed from home and friends.

But with her dying breath she whispered: "It makes little difference where you bury my body. The only thing I ask of you both is that, no matter where you are, you remember me at the altar of God."

Breathing became more difficult and soon St. Monica passed to God.    Augustine, the boy of her prayers and tears, later became the great St. Augustine.

### Do You Understand This Story?

1. What lesson did Monica learn soon after her marriage?
2. Why did the boy Augustine grieve his mother?
3. What did he do that almost broke her heart?
4. Why was Augustine banished from home?
5. What did the bishop say that gave hope to St. Monica?
6. Why did St. Monica follow her son to Rome and Milan?
7. How was Augustine converted?
8. What lesson does the life of St. Monica teach us?

# ST. PATRICK, THE APOSTLE OF IRELAND

(*About 373–493*)

## 1. THE CHRISTIAN SLAVE

A frantic Scotch youth struggled violently with savage pirates as they bound and gagged him. His cries were answered with vile curses and threats and his struggle was of no avail. The pirates quickly overcame him and the poor boy was dragged into their sailboat, where he was thrown upon the plunder that these wicked men had stolen. Sails were quickly hoisted. Strong arms grasped the clumsy oars and the boat was soon cutting the waves for the coast of Ireland. All this happened many hundreds of years ago — toward the end of the fourth century — but it is of interest to us to-day because the captive was St. Patrick.

The boat was tossed hither and thither on the choppy sea. The sunburned, muscular bodies of the sailors moved back and forth as they splashed the oars into the foaming waves. The captive boy was not accustomed to the rough sea and the motion made him ill. The rugged pirates laughed. They loved the wild waves and were thrilled to battle with them.

The sea became smoother as the boat neared the coast. The sailors drew in their oars and watched the big sails carry the boat to shore.

Patrick was too ill to stand up and see the island toward which they were sailing. It was a beautiful mass of green jutting out of the sea. Rocky cliffs, low, rolling hills, and long stretches of level land basked in the warm rays of the sun. Before the heartbroken boy realized it, the boat was drifting in the shallow water near the shore. The youth and the plunder were taken ashore and Patrick set his foot for the first time on Ireland.

The lad was soon sold as a slave to an Irish chieftain. In his home in Scotland, he had had slaves at his command, and now he was forced to tend the cattle of a harsh master. It was dreary and lonesome to live on the hills and in the valleys with no companions except the cattle. No voice but the scolding tones of a pagan master sounded in his ears. No kind face ever smiled upon him. Alone, all alone in exile, he spent his days and nights with the cows and sheep.

Yet, he was not alone. During those six years he lived in the closest friendship with God. Daily he led his flocks and herds to rich pastures either in the fertile valley or on the grassy highlands. As the cattle lazily browsed in the fields, St. Patrick prayed to God. He learned to love prayer and spoke to his heavenly Father like a faithful devoted child. He pitied the pagans about him who had never heard of the great God Who made the heavens and the earth. The magic of their pagan priests made him shudder. His youthful spirit begged God to have mercy on this poor people and bring them to the light of the true faith.

## 2. The Escape from Slavery

For six long years, Patrick tended the sheep of his pagan master. Then, in a wonderful manner, those days of slavery were ended. God inspired him to flee to a distant part of the coast and board a boat riding at anchor. The thought of home and friends gave him increased strength to hasten to his journey's end.

A few weeks afterward, St. Patrick was back at his old home, embracing the devoted mother who had mourned him as dead. It was pleasant to be back again, free and happy, to receive the greetings of friends and relatives.

But strange to say, Patrick had left his heart in Ireland. His mind frequently turned to the hills and valleys where he had wandered as a shepherd slave. He had always thought that there was much good in the Irish character, although he had been shown little kindness in Ireland. He pitied the people because they had not heard of the Christ Who came to save all mankind. He longed for the day when God would send someone to preach the true faith in that pagan land.

As the years passed on, a yearning to return to Ireland stirred in Patrick's heart. The cry of the Irish souls for the faith of Christ echoed and reëchoed in his ears. These pagan people seemed to beg for someone to break to them the Bread of Life, but for years their cry had gone unanswered.

### 3. The Missionary to Ireland

Almost forty years had passed since the days of St. Patrick's slavery in Ireland. As an old man of sixty years, he determined to answer that cry from across the sea. He journeyed to Rome and asked the pope to send him to convert the Irish. The Holy Father looked at the bearded old man pleading for permission to convert a sturdy pagan race. He was struck by Patrick's zeal and enthusiasm. He knew that the grace of God was working in Patrick's heart.

The pope ordained him a priest and then consecrated him bishop, the first bishop of Ireland.

"Go forth, Patrick," he said, "and preach to the Irish the gospel of Jesus Christ. May God's grace be with you and may He crown your every effort with success."

Patrick lost no time in getting to the land of his future labors. Some forty years before, he had been brought an unwilling captive to those shores, and now he was returning there for the love of God and the salvation of souls. He exiled himself to bring to those pagan hearts the teachings of Jesus — to bring the Irish into God's friendly circle. Neither the love of kindred nor the tears of friends nor the opposition of those who blamed him could overcome St. Patrick's love for souls. He bade farewell to all — home, friends, native land — for His Master's sake, and chose to live a wanderer and an exile in a strange land for the love of the heavenly kingdom.

Armed with the cross and filled with holy zeal, St. Patrick again landed on the coast of Ireland. He returned not as a slave bound in chains but as a bishop, a captain in the army of the Lord. He began his victorious march through Ireland, preaching the doctrine of Christ and receiving converts into the church.

### 4. PATRICK FACES THE ENEMY

As Easter drew near, Patrick planned a bold stroke. He knew that the Irish king, the chieftains, and throngs of people would be gathered on the hill of Tara for the great pagan feast that was celebrated at the same time as our Easter. The pagan Druid priests would be there to show their powers of magic and to light the great fire that began the celebration. The evening before, all the fires in Ireland had to be put out. No fire was permitted under penalty of death until the pagan priests had started the fire on the hill of Tara.

St. Patrick decided to carry the war into the very camp of the enemy. With a few faithful friends, he proceeded to a hill a short distance from Tara. There, on the day before Easter, St. Patrick lighted the Easter fire of the Christians. A large quantity of dried tree boughs was piled upon the fire. The red flames rose high. The higher they leaped, the more pleased Patrick was. He wanted the king and the Druids on the hill of Tara to see the fire.

His wish was granted. The king and his chieftains gazed angrily at the flames. They wondered who would dare to disobey the sacred laws of the land. Death must be the offender's doom.

The old Druid priests knew what the fire meant. They told the king that unless the fire was put out now, it could never be put out. In the fire they saw the flame of the faith of Christ and they knew that if its first light were not quenched, it would spread over all the land. The king sent soldiers to bring the culprit before the throne. In chariots drawn by swift steeds, they dashed down the hill, across the valley, and up to the place where St. Patrick was quietly watching the flames. They requested Patrick to follow them to the king. He was delighted. His opportunity had come at last.

ST. PATRICK PREACHES BEFORE THE KING

Fearlessly St. Patrick advanced to the king. The chiefs were compelled to admire his bravery. The king questioned him about the fire. He admitted that he had started the fire although he knew that the law forbade it. This daring speech amazed those who heard it. Patrick then explained that all who believe in the true God, the great God of the Christians, light the holy fire on the day before Easter.

The pagans laughed at him and asked: "Who is the great God you talk about? What wonders can He do?" They boasted of the magic powers of their priests and asked St. Patrick to prove that his God was more powerful.

## 5. Patrick's Victories

The apostle of Christ gladly accepted the challenge. The Druids showed their magic, but St. Patrick followed each of their efforts with something more wonderful. This so enraged the king and chieftains that they decided to put Patrick to death.

The saint read their thoughts. He prayed to God for help. Darkness suddenly fell upon the hill and an earthquake shook the earth. St. Patrick and his friends escaped in the dark.

But the very next day St. Patrick again appeared before the king and the chieftains. He told them of the great God Who made the world. He spoke of the death of the Son of God on the cross for the love of men.

The king was indignant at the boldness of **Patrick** and planned to poison him. Pretending to be friendly, he invited Patrick to dinner. A cup of poison was offered to the saint. He suspected the evil intention of the king and made the sign of the cross over the cup. Then he put it to his lips and drank the poison without harm. Once again God had protected one of his servants.

Thus far St. Patrick had been victorious but the pagan chieftains were not convinced of the truth of his teachings. They demanded that Patrick and the Druid priests test their powers in another contest. Patrick readily agreed, but the pagan priests feared defeat and gave their consent unwillingly.

Two piles of wood were prepared, one of dry twigs and the other of green saplings. A pagan boy was wrapped in St. Patrick's cloak and placed on the green twigs. The Druids thought that the green saplings would not burn. A Christian boy was wrapped in the white robe of the Druids and placed upon the dry wood. The Druids insisted on changing the cloaks in order to deceive the Christian God.

Soldiers applied the torch to both piles of wood. The dry wood with the Christian boy refused to burn. Again and again, the torches were applied to it without result.  Once a small flame burst forth and burned the pagan robe that was wrapped about the boy, but the child was left unharmed.  However, the green saplings blazed forth and burned the pagan boy to death.

St. Patrick's cloak was found among the ashes, covered with dirt but not burned.  This miracle again filled the hearts of the chieftains with murder and God saved His apostle with another earthquake.

### 6. Paganism Conquered

The king and his advisers, however, saw that it was useless to oppose Patrick any longer.  He was given permission to preach his gospel wherever he desired.  St. Patrick did not wish to lose the advantage he had gained over the pagan priests in the recent contests.  He remained, therefore, for several days on the hill of Tara, preaching and converting many to the new faith.  On that now famous hill, St. Patrick conquered paganism.  He had broken its power over the people when he showed that the God of Whom he spoke was greater and more powerful than all the Druid priests in Ireland.

From Tara, Patrick set out to preach in every part of Ireland.  He went from north to south, from east to west.  Wherever his voice was heard, the pagan priests fled and the people fell down before him.  He ordained many holy priests and consecrated bishops to help him in his work. He established convents and hundreds of pious Irish maidens entered them, to pray for God's blessing on the people of Ireland.

At the age of one hundred and twenty years, after having spent sixty years in Ireland, St. Patrick died. He left a flourishing church, filled with faithful Christians and governed by holy men who continued the great work of the first apostle of Ireland. The story of Patrick's success is a beautiful story of the conversion of a whole nation by the zeal of one man without the shedding of a drop of blood.

### QUESTIONS

1. How did the boy Patrick happen to be in Ireland?
2. After his escape, why did he wish to return?
3. Why was there so much trouble over the fire on the hill of Tara?
4. How did St. Patrick show the Irish that the God about whom he spoke was greater than all the pagan priests in Ireland?
5. Tell the story of the conversion of Ireland.

# SAINT COLUMBA

(521–597)

## 1. EXILED FROM HOME

The cold waters of the Irish Sea splashed over the moss-covered crags that lay along the shore. Long, narrow, skin-lined boats, fastened to the beach with ropes, were tossed to and fro by the waves. A little group of sad monks knelt in prayer at the water's edge. It was their last prayer on the land they loved. They had just bade farewell to home and friends and were about to leave Ireland forever. Columba, their master, was being banished from the land of his birth and they were to accompany him in exile.

Columba's heart was sad, indeed. It was his anger and longing for revenge that had brought bloodshed and death to the Irish clans. The king of Tara had insulted him and the monk had demanded that his friends declare war upon this ruler. He had even gone so far as to encourage the fighters on the battlefield itself. His fiery temper, that he had so often tried to control, had brought sorrow to many an Irish home.

Now he was being punished for it. The leaders in the Irish church pitied him. They knew of the won-

ST. COLUMBA AND HIS FRIENDS LEAVE IRELAND

derful work he had done in building monasteries and gathering monks about him to praise and honor God. They knew, too, that the people loved and admired him. But his quick temper had led him to commit this terrible sin and he must do penance for it, so it had been decided that he must spend the rest of his life as an exile working for the conversion of pagan souls.

Was it any wonder, then, that Columba's heart was sad? He was deeply fond of his native land. He loved its people, its rolling hills, and shaded valleys. To him it was the dearest place on earth.

After kissing the sandy beach, the doomed man rose from his prayers and led his faithful companions to the boats. Rough oars were used to push the boats into the deep water. The monks quickly hoisted the crude sails and soon they were sailing over the choppy waves.

Farther and farther along the bosom of the sea they went. The eyes of Columba were fastened upon the disappearing hills of Ireland, which grew gradually smaller until finally they seemed to sink into the water. Ireland, his beloved Ireland, was gone forever.

## 2. Columba at Iona

Columba looked about him. Foamy waves of blue-green water greeted him on all sides. He gazed into the cloudless sky and began to pray: "O God, Creator of heaven and earth, I beseech Thee to direct our course. Lead us to that shore where we may give most honor and glory to Thy holy name. Guide us to those who have never heard the sweet name of Jesus nor the story of His sacrifice for men. Give us courage and strength to bear our cross in meekness and patience.''

On and on through the rough sea they rowed. The strong arms of the monks sent the oars through angry waves and forced the boats forward. It was no easy task to battle the waves, and the monks knew that their strength could not last forever. They hoped that land would soon appear. Before long their prayer was answered and the exhausted monks found themselves gliding into the shallow waters along the rocky coast of the Isle of Iona.

This bleak, barren island was to be the home of Columba and his monks for the rest of their lives. On the side of a mountain they built for themselves little huts or cells made of willow twigs and covered with skins and ivy.

High above the others was the cell of Columba. A stone was his pillow and the earth was his bed. When not working in the fields or preaching to the natives, he prayed, wrote, and slept in this crude home.

But it was indeed a happy and holy family of monks that St. Columba guided as a father and friend. At the middle of the night and several times during the day, they gathered in the simple chapel to sing the praises of the God they loved so well.

### 3. Missionaries from Iona

Before long St. Columba felt that the time had come when he should send his monks as missionaries to the natives. Alone or by twos, they left their island home to preach the gospel of Christ to the pagan people of Scotland and northern England. Their saintly lives and glowing zeal brought thousands and thousands into the church of God.

Columba, the good master, always led the way. No task was too difficult, no tribe too hostile, no journey too long. He was the good shepherd who guided and protected his sheep. All the strength of his mind and heart was devoted to serving God and bringing souls to Him.

Soon the little Isle of Iona became famous. People came from far and near to seek the advice and blessing of the holy Columba. Many wished to join his monks and serve God under his guidance. He trained his new disciples with the zeal and love of a father and then sent them forth to build other monasteries and spread the faith of Christ. It is said that St. Columba and his monks established more than three hundred monasteries during his lifetime.

## 4. THE CONQUERED TEMPER

Often when Columba's thoughts wandered across the sea to the land of his birth, he shed tears of bitter sorrow and penance for the things that his quick temper had caused him to do. He knew that it had been the greatest fault in his character. It had ruined the early part of his life and had brought him disgrace and sorrow.

Daily he had prayed to Jesus to make his heart meek and humble like the divine Heart that loved men so much, and now, by prayer and penance on the barren Isle of Iona, he had conquered his fiery temper.

Columba the abbot of Iona was far different from Columba the fiery-tempered monk of Ireland. He had become the humblest and meekest of men and was loved for his gentleness by all who knew him.

Year followed year, and Columba worked and prayed till in old age he became too weak to leave his homely cell. He quietly awaited death.

Sorrowing monks who had looked upon him as a kind and loving father knelt at his side as he breathed his last before the altar in the hillside chapel on the little island. This was long ago on a midnight in June of the year 597, but Columba's name is still remembered and honored wherever God's saints are known.

## Study Helps

1. Give a new title to this story.
2. Into what two parts can the story be easily divided?
3. Compare the character of Columba in Ireland and at Iona.
4. What great sin did Columba commit in Ireland?
5. What fault in his character caused this?
6. How did Columba conquer this fault?
7. Could Columba be called a saint while in Ireland?   Why?
8. How can we overcome a bad temper?

# SAINT BONIFACE

(*680–755*)

## 1. A CHILD'S DESIRE

A golden-haired boy threw his arms around the tanned neck of his father, who sat dozing before the fireplace in the hall of a great, English house. He kissed the bearded face and roused the father from his dreams.

"Father," he said, "when I grow to be a big man, I am going to be a Benedictine monk. I'll go around the whole world and preach about our Lord." The boy looked into the weather-beaten face of his father and saw that he was displeased.

"You are too young to be thinking about such things," said the father sternly. "Put such thoughts out of your head. When you grow to be a man, you are to take my place as the head of this house and the owner of these great farmlands and orchards."

Little Winfrid was sad and a tiny tear stole down his fat, rosy cheek. In his boyish heart, he knew that he did not want to own great castles and large stretches of land. He wanted to be like the monks that he had seen traveling through the country, telling the people about God. That night as the boy knelt beside his bed, he opened his heart to his heavenly Father and asked His help.

## 2. THE HUNTER

Year followed year, and Winfrid grew into a strong, bright lad who loved to join his playmates as they scampered over hill and valley or climbed the trees in the orchard seeking the reddest and sweetest apples. When the older folks rode forth on a deer hunt or rabbit chase, Winfrid was always mounted on his grey pony, ready to dash through the woods with the leaders.

His father was proud of these manly traits and often encouraged his son to join in the hunt. Whenever the arrow from Winfrid's bow struck a fleeing rabbit or brought a wild duck to the ground, the father would reward his son with a coin or a promise of something the boy wanted.

But during these years of happiness, one thought was ever present in the mind of Winfrid — the thought that one day he was going to be a priest. He had never changed his mind since that evening many years before when he first spoke about it to his father. The time was now drawing near when he must begin to prepare himself for his high calling.

### 3. The Father's Decision

One chilly day, Winfrid and his father were alone again in the living room of the homestead. The boy was now about fourteen years old, but tall and muscular beyond his years. He poked the fire with an iron rod and caused crackling sparks to fly about the old copper kettle that hung over the fireplace. Then he drew a crude, wooden bench near the fire and looked anxiously into the face of his father.

The father knew that something was on the boy's mind. "Well, my lad," he said, "you look troubled. What is the matter?"

"Nothing is wrong, Father, but I want to speak to you about my future," answered Winfrid.

The father looked closely into the face of his son. "You know, Winfrid, that I am as deeply interested in that future as you are. You need have no worries. All my wealth and property will be yours. You can soon marry some fair maiden and with her you will live happily here after your poor father is dead."

"But, Father," protested the boy, "those are not the plans I have decided upon. I do not wish to be the wealthy master of your estates. I have no desire to get married. Since the night long ago that I spoke to you in this very room, I have had no other thought than the one I spoke of then. I intend to be a priest.

To-night I ask your permission to study at the monastery."

The father was beside himself with rage. In his anger he reached for a cane to strike his son but the chair overturned and sent the furious man reeling upon the floor. Winfrid was at his side instantly and helped him to his feet. The father stamped up and down the room like a wild lion in a cage.

"A priest!" he yelled. "No son of mine will ever be a priest! I would sooner see you dead. Banish the thought forever from your mind. Out! Out! before I trounce you."

The boy saw that arguing was useless. He left the room, snatching his cap and cloak as he went. The door closed behind him and he set out toward the forest. He soon found himself wandering beneath large oak and spreading maple trees, whose leaves were tinged with the golden brown of early autumn.

"O God," he prayed, as he walked along, "soften the heart of my father that he may see the right. Let him know that I am answering Your call to labor for the souls of men."

On his return home, no mention was made of the scene before the fireplace. The father was delighted with the thought that he had put an end to his son's vocation. But God's call in the heart of his boy was not to be cast aside so easily.

## 4. THE FATHER CHANGES HIS MIND

Autumn faded into winter with its heavy snows and cold rains. Winfrid's father returned late one night after a rabbit hunt. A downpour of sleet and rain had drenched him through and through. Shivering with chills, he gruffly ordered the servants to make him a hot drink. Fresh wood was thrown upon the fire and the red, leaping flames brightened the room. The master drew his chair near the fire but the chills continued. At last, the servants helped him to his room.

All that night and for many days and nights afterward, he tossed upon his bed, now burning with fever, now shivering with chills. At his side always stood Winfrid, ever ready to help him. The sick man moaned in his pain: "Oh, it is the punishment of God upon me. Forgive me, O Lord, but I love him."

For days the nurses and his family heard him repeat this remark over and over again. They thought that his mind was wandering because of the fever and paid little attention to what he was saying.

Finally, one day as Winfrid handed him a drink, he began to weep. "O my boy," he sobbed, "God has punished me for what I have done to you. God has called you to be a priest and I have kept you from answering that call. Go now, my son, with your father's blessing. Prepare yourself to serve your Lord. And when my body is dust in yonder grave-yard, remember my poor soul at the altar of the living God."

With tear-stained face, Winfrid bent over to kiss the fevered brow of his beloved father. He knew now that it was a father's love, mistaken though it was, that had spoken on those two nights in the room below.

The fever seemed suddenly to leave the sick man after the kiss of his son. In a few days, the master was walking about again.

## 5. The Benedictine Missionary

Winfrid joined the Benedictine monks and took up their life of study, work, and prayer. The youth was happy in his new home, happy in the thought that soon he would be a leader in the army of God. Time passed quickly and, almost before he knew it, he was ordained a priest. For some years he labored in England, but his mind always wandered across the northern seas to the land where the fair-haired Germans lived.

The abbot who ruled the monastery in which Winfrid lived granted him permission to labor among the German people. Through the little hamlets and towns he traveled, preaching wherever he went. His efforts met with small success. He was driven out of some towns, and in others the people refused to listen to him.

The holy monk returned to England but he did not give up his hope of winning the German people to the cause of Christ. In a few years he was kneeling before the Holy Father and receiving his blessing before going back to Germany. With renewed zeal, he again took up his work among the Germans, and now his efforts were crowned with success. Tribe after tribe became converted and was baptized. The saint went north, south, east, and west, planting the cross of Christ over a little church in every town and, wherever possible, opening a school.

### 6. WINFRID BECOMES BISHOP BONIFACE

The pope was delighted with Winfrid's success. He called the missionary to Rome and consecrated him bishop. "You will henceforth be called Boniface instead of Winfrid," said the pope. "Go back to your people with God's blessing. Keep up the good work and our Lord will reward you a hundredfold."

Back again to his flock Bishop Boniface went. It was a long, tiresome journey on foot from Italy to Germany, but hardships have never stood in the way of God's saints.

Boniface continued his labors in spreading the faith, building churches, monasteries, and schools throughout the land.   England answered his appeals for priests and nuns by sending over to Germany many saints and scholars to instruct the children of this noble race.

Almost forty years had passed since Bishop Boniface first began his labors among the Germans.   These had been years of trials and sufferings, but they had been happy years because they were given to the Lord. The cold blasts of northern winters had chilled the body of St. Boniface but nothing had ever cooled his love for the people among whom he lived.   With the years, his hair had turned to snowy white; his face was lined with wrinkles; and his pace had become slow. But in spite of these signs of age, no one would have suspected that the bishop was seventy-five years old.

His duties as bishop kept him more or less in the neighborhood of the cathedral city of Mainz.   In spite of all the work he had done in bringing numberless converts into the church, the apostle was not satisfied. The Frisians along the North Sea still remained outside the fold.   It was among these people that Boniface had first begun his missionary work.   Now he decided to finish his labors by making another effort to win this warlike people to Christ.

## 7. CROWNED A MARTYR

He resigned as bishop and set out with fifty-two companions to work along the shores of the North Sea.

ST. BONIFACE PRAYS JUST BEFORE DEATH

His efforts now met with success. Many of the members of the tribe were prepared for baptism. On the day appointed for bringing these latest converts into the church, St. Boniface and his companions were awaiting their arrival at the banks of a river.

Suddenly they beheld a hostile pagan tribe rushing through the woods toward the camp. Their bows and arrows and shining spears showed that they came as enemies, not as friends. With the river behind them and the forest before them, there was no escape for the missionaries. They cried out to Boniface for help.

The white-haired old man stood in the midst of them like a true soldier of Christ. He saw the savage horde approaching. Their fierce shouts and shrieks echoed through the woods. Nearer and nearer came the messengers of death.

The companions of Boniface knelt about him. He raised his crucifix on high and with the sign of the cross solemnly pronounced the words of absolution over the bowed heads.

Then extending his hands, he prayed in a firm, clear voice: "O Lord Jesus Christ, God of the living and the dead, we commend our souls to Thee and implore Thee to receive us into the company of Thy holy saints. Remember, O Lord, that we are Thy servants, servants who have been loyal and true to Thee during life. For the glory of Thy holy name, we have left home and friends to spend our days in pagan lands.

"Remember not, O Lord, our sins by which we may have offended Thy divine Majesty, but be mindful of us in Thy heavenly kingdom. Draw wide the gates of heaven for us and let Thy chosen martyrs conduct us to our eternal home.

"O dearest Mother Mary, watch over us in this our hour of triumph. Guide us to the throne of Thy —"

St. Boniface never finished his prayer. A shower of poisoned darts from the enemy struck him and he fell lifeless in the midst of his companions. The brutal pagans dashed furiously upon the kneeling Christians and fifty-two martyrs with their leader joined the ranks of God's chosen ones.

### Answer These

1. What happened when Winfrid first told his father that he wanted to be a priest?
2. How did Winfrid enjoy himself as a boy?
3. What do you think about his second interview with his father?
4. Why did the father think that Winfrid had changed his mind?
5. How did the father happen to give his consent?
6. How did the Germans at first receive Winfrid?
7. Where did he get the name Boniface?
8. Tell the story of the death of St. Boniface.

# SAINT THOMAS A BECKET

*(1117–1170)*

## 1. HAWKING

A group of men walked gayly toward the hitching posts where their horses were restlessly pawing the ground. Laughing and chatting, they jumped into their saddles. The spirited horses cantered across the meadows to the woods that stretched for miles along the river.

Each rider wore a heavy gauntlet on his left hand and to his wrist was fastened a trained hawk. The party was setting out for a day of hawking, as the English sport of hunting birds or game with the help of a hawk is called.

The thud of the horses' hoofs sent many a pheasant flying up from its nest in fear. As the birds fluttered and hovered around their woodland homes, the trained hawks darted from the arms of the hunters. The hawks caught the birds in their powerful claws, then returned in triumph to their owners.

There was little sport, however, in bringing down the gentle pheasant. The hunters spurred their horses onward to the marshy swamplands where the wild duck made its home.

Thomas à Becket was one of the young men who had set off so gayly. Now as he rode along, he caught a glimpse of a wild duck sailing through the air, high above the tips of the oak and cypress trees. For several minutes it glided in circles above him. He jumped from his horse and ran to an open space in the woods so that his hawk could catch sight of the duck. In a flash, the keen eye of the hunting bird saw its victim. It rustled its wings for a moment and then, like an arrow from a bow, it soared straight for the duck.

As soon as the wild duck saw its enemy flying toward it, it wheeled around and dived for the water two hundred feet below. The hawk saw this move and made a desperate effort to swoop down upon the duck. Splash! The duck landed in the water near the bank and began to swim quickly toward the middle of the river. It had no fear now of the claw of its pursuer.

The hawk was disappointed. Very few birds had ever escaped from it before. It decided to catch the duck at any cost. Down it swooped upon its prey in the water. The birds struggled for a few minutes. Then the duck dived under the water and left the hawk fluttering around on the top.

## 2. Down the Stream

With dismay, Thomas watched this scene from the bank. He called to his hawk, but the struggling bird could not raise itself from the water. The bird was too valuable to lose. Holding the long bough of a tree in his hand, Thomas waded into the stream. Alas! he went too far and was carried down the river by the swift current.

His clothes became soaked with water and it was impossible for him to swim. In vain did he strive to reach the shore. On and on he was swept until the river narrowed just before passing a large mill. The great wooden paddles of the mill wheel were whirled around by the water as it dashed by. He knew that if a paddle ever struck him it would kill him. Death stared Thomas in the face. He prayed to God to save him.

"O God, come to my help. Save me from death," he repeated over and over again.

God heard his prayer. Just before he arrived at the mill, the paddle wheel stopped. Reaching for one of the paddles, he grabbed it and held fast until one of the mill hands rescued him.

## 3. The Lord High Chancellor

That night a very thankful young man said his prayers with more fervor than usual. As he faced

death in the river, he had realized that thus far his life
had been useless both to himself and to God.   His
days had been spent in hunting and riding, his evenings
in dancing and feasting.   He resolved now to change
his life, to make it useful to God, to himself, and to his
fellow men.

He was no longer seen following the chase.   The banquet halls of the country missed his cheerful face.   He
cut himself off from his idle companions.   He attached
himself to the household of the archbishop of Canterbury and was soon given the position of secretary.

His ability and piety won the favor of those about
him.   Even the king admired the talent of the former
sportsman.   At different times, Thomas was sent to
Europe on important business for both the king and
the archbishop.   So faithfully did he perform his
duties, that he was promoted from position to position
until finally he was made lord high chancellor of England, the most important office in the kingdom.

Honors and power, however, did not change his
character.   He always remained the kind, humble
man who had entered the service of the archbishop
some years before.

### 4. ARCHBISHOP OF CANTERBURY

On the death of the archbishop of Canterbury, King
Henry insisted that his friend and advisor, Thomas à

Becket, be made archbishop. The lord chancellor refused the honor. He felt that he was unworthy to hold such a high position in God's church. The king remained firm in his demand. Thomas pleaded with him to appoint someone else. He clearly foresaw all the difficulties that would arise.

"Most gracious majesty," he said to the king, "should God permit me to be archbishop of Canterbury, I should soon lose your Majesty's friendship. The love with which you now honor me would be turned to hatred. You would ask me to permit you to do things against the interests of God's church, which I could not and would not grant. My enemies would then try to make this appear as a crime in order to make me lose your favor."

The king paid no heed to this honest protest. Much against his will, Thomas was forced to accept the new dignity of archbishop of Canterbury.

Up to this time, Thomas had been lord chancellor of England but he was not a priest. Therefore, in a solemn ceremony he was first ordained to the holy priesthood and later consecrated bishop.

## 5. DEFENDER OF THE CHURCH

Archbishop Becket was now a changed man. He set aside the gorgeous robes of the lord chancellor. As a penance he wore next his skin a coarse hair shirt.

This was covered by a simple, black habit like the one the Benedictines use. Each morning at two o'clock he arose to chant the morning prayers of the church with the other priests and monks of his household. It is said that daily he washed the feet of thirteen beggars in memory of the time when our Lord washed the feet of His disciples. With his own hands he fed the poor and the hungry who came to his door.

Henry did not like the idea of this change in the life of his friend, the lord chancellor. A worldly bishop was more to his taste. He wanted a bishop who would do as the king wished without regard to the rights of the church. He desired a weakling who would obey his will.

But much to his sorrow, Henry found that the new archbishop was not that kind of man. The first offense was given when Thomas resigned the position of chancellor.

"It is impossible," he said, "for a man to be the defender of the rights of the church and at the same time the advisor of a king who tries to abuse those rights." It was thus that St. Thomas threatened war on his king.

The archbishop brought up the question of appointing bishops. In those days the church permitted the king to appoint the bishops. Very often, when a bishop died, the king would refuse to appoint his successor for a year or two. During the time of the vacancy, the king would do as he pleased with the church property.

When St. Thomas became archbishop, several places were without bishops. He asked the king to appoint them, but Henry refused. Thomas explained that Henry had no right to rob the churches as he had been doing. He tried to show the king the injury that he was doing to religion. Henry argued and refused. Then he promised and delayed. But finally after months of quarreling, the king gave in and appointed the bishops.

Other arguments arose between Henry and Thomas when the king tried to injure the rights of the church. St. Thomas bravely defended these rights and refused to yield an inch to the unjust commands of the king.

On the advice of some of the nobles, Henry sent an edict through the kingdom, commanding every bishop to take an oath to respect the "customs of the kingdom." The archbishop, having been chancellor for a number of years, knew that many of these customs were unlawful and unjust. They were dangerous to the peace and welfare of the church. Therefore, he refused to take the oath unless the king added the words "as far as is lawful and just."

This defiant refusal angered Henry. He called a meeting of the nobles and bishops. Here he condemned Thomas and deprived him of his possessions. Some of the archbishop's friends begged him to resign and save himself.

This suggestion offended the holy man. "To do what you suggest," he said, "would be to betray the truth and to be disloyal to the cause of God's church. I am willing, if need be, to defend both with my life. When there is a question of justice and rights, I fear the threats and punishments of no earthly king."

## 6. IN EXILE

Matters daily grew worse. The king planned all sorts of ways of persecuting Thomas. The saint finally decided to place the matter before the pope, who was then in France. Secretly he crossed the Channel. Little did he dream as he landed on that friendly shore that several years would pass before he returned to his beloved Canterbury.

The pope listened with eagerness to the story of the king's attempt to rob and ruin the church. "Be loyal to your trust," he said, "and God will guide you." The French king pitied the exile and offered him money and lodging. Wandering from town to town, resting here for a few weeks and there for a few months, the archbishop traveled through France.

Weeks turned into months and months into years. Still the holy man wandered in exile. Several times the pope and the king of France tried to settle the quarrel between Henry and Thomas. The king never seemed to be sincere and the archbishop justly doubted his promises.

Finally, the king journeyed to France to meet St. Thomas. He invited the exile back to England, promising that everything would be settled properly.

### 7. BACK AGAIN IN ENGLAND

St. Thomas returned to England, although God had warned him that he would be put to death. Scarcely had the poor man landed in his native land when some of his enemies began to plot against him. By fair means or foul, they were determined to get rid of the saint.

They secretly approached the king and said to him: "Your majesty, there will be no peace in your kingdom while the traitor of Canterbury lives. You know only too well how much the people love him. With a word he could turn the whole kingdom against you. Your crown will never be secure upon your head until Thomas of Canterbury is no more."

This message had the desired effect. It roused the anger of the king to the exploding point. He cursed his nobles. He cursed his servants. He cursed everybody near him.

"You have feasted at my table," he said sharply to

the nobles. "You have been enriched by my gifts. Yet not one of you is man enough to rid me of this bishop who is more trouble to me than all the people in my kingdom."

## 8. THE CROWN OF MARTYRDOM

This was what the nobles wanted — the royal permission to kill St. Thomas. They armed themselves with swords and spears and brought several companions to the archbishop's home.

St. Thomas with the other priests of the household was in the church chanting vespers. The last rays of the evening sun lit up the beautiful stained-glass windows and cast warm, rich shadows on the stone floor. Candles burned dimly in bronze candlesticks on the marble altar. Clouds of fragrant incense moved silently about the sanctuary. The musical roll of men's deep voices chanting the psalms of David echoed through the church.

This prayerful scene should have inspired faith and awe in any Christian heart. But the hearts of the wicked nobles were not touched. With their swords and spears in hand, they dashed up the middle of the church, yelling: "Death to the traitor! The traitor! Where is the traitor?"

The chanting stopped suddenly. The startled monks looked around and saw a small army of soldiers and

ST. THOMAS À BECKET FACES HIS ENEMIES

nobles, armed as if for battle. Into the sanctuary
raced the murderers, repeating their cry, "Where is
the traitor?"

No answer came from the frightened monks.

Then one of the nobles asked, "Where is the archbishop?"

Thomas stepped forward and looked defiantly at his
murderers. "The archbishop stands before you," he
said, "but he is no traitor. There is no more loyal
heart in the kingdom than the heart of Thomas à
Becket. No man ever loved his country and his king
more than I."

The monks and the members of his household fled
in fear, leaving the brave archbishop to face his enemies
alone.

"You have taunted our king long enough," sneered
one of the nobles. "You have seen the sun set for the
last time. To-night you must die."

"To die for God, for justice, and for the liberty of
the church, will be the greatest joy of my life. I have
fought for God's holy church with all the powers of
my body and soul and I shall be glad to die fighting
on the field of honor. Take my life if you will, but
spare my friends." The poor man had little need to
plead for his friends because they all had deserted him
and sought safety in flight.

The heroic defender of the church then knelt upon

the floor before the altar and stretched forth his hands to heaven in prayer.

"O almighty and merciful Father, my hour is now come. I have served Thee faithfully in life, and in death I offer myself to Thee. Have mercy on my poor soul. Pardon all the sins by which I may have offended Thy divine Majesty. Forgive my enemies and those who now seek my life. Pardon them, O Father of mercies, because they know not what they do."

The ruffians could not wait till the doomed man had finished his prayer. One after another, heavy blows from their swords struck the head of St. Thomas. He fell back unconscious. The wicked nobles wanted to be sure of his death. One of them crushed the skull of their victim with the hilt of his sword while another pierced his heart with a spear. Blood gushed from the wounds of the saint and covered the floor. The pallor of death spread over the face of the saint as the soul of St. Thomas à Becket, the loyal defender of God's church, was welcomed into heaven.

St. Thomas by his death accomplished what he could not do in life. All England was enraged at the brutal death of its beloved friend and protector. The king was struck with remorse and wept bitterly over the murder of his former friend and chancellor. He made a pilgrimage to Thomas's tomb and before the shrine took an oath that he would restore the rights and the liberty of the church. The blood of the martyr thus loosed the chains that bound the church of Christ in England.

SOMETHING TO DO

Number a paper from 1 to 20. After each number, write the name of the person or thing described by the corresponding word.

| | | | |
|---|---|---|---|
| 1. | well-groomed | 11. | thirteen |
| 2. | trained | 12. | defiant |
| 3. | timid | 13. | friendly |
| 4. | keen | 14. | native |
| 5. | swooped | 15. | exploding |
| 6. | struggling | 16. | evening |
| 7. | thankful | 17. | startled |
| 8. | humble | 18. | loyal |
| 9. | honest | 19. | doomed |
| 10. | gorgeous | 20. | brutal |

# SAINT FRANCIS OF ASSISI

## (1182–1226)

## 1. A GAY YOUTH

The handsome Francis Bernadone was one of the leaders of the gallant youth of Assisi.  He was a jolly lad who liked good times and fine clothes.  The brightest and the gayest colors were never too flashy for him.  The people of Assisi, especially the young ladies, often paused on the street to look at him as he passed by, dressed in his satin tunic and with his mantle thrown carelessly over his shoulder.  No party for the young folks of the town was ever complete unless the hearty laugh and the cheerful voice of Francis joined in the merrymaking.

He loved adventure and he was thrilled with the stories of brave knights and fair ladies.  The bold, daring hero who faced death to rescue some charming maiden was his idol.  Tales of bravery on the battlefield also interested him.  He would sit by the hour in his father's store or before some tavern as the old men of the town spoke of the great warriors of Assisi in the days gone by.  A secret yearning to be a soldier burned in the heart of Francis.

The chance soon presented itself when war was declared between Assisi and Perugia, a fortified town some miles distant. Francis put on a soldier's uniform and hastened to the defense of his beloved Assisi. With mingled feelings of pride and bravery, he rode forth to join the army that had encamped outside the walls of the city.

The fighting began — cruel, bloody fighting. The enemy made a surprise attack. Francis, with several of his companions, was captured. Alas! his hopes were blasted. The daring youth who desired to be a hero was shamefully cast into the prison of the enemy.

But this sad turn of events did not crush his spirits. He remained happy in his gloomy prison and did his best to cheer his downhearted companions. The captives were freed in a year and received a royal welcome on returning to their native city.

## 2. A CHANGE FOR THE BETTER

The poor food and the weary months in prison had weakened Francis. On his return home, a serious illness attacked him. For several days he hung between life and death; then slowly he began to improve. The color gradually came back to his thin, pale cheeks and his winning smile began to play about his face. It was many days, however, before he appeared on the streets of Assisi.

When he did, he was not the Francis of the days of old, the youth who craved for jolly times and fine clothes. God had opened his eyes during his illness and he saw the uselessness of the life he had been leading, a selfish life given over to pleasure and the wasting of money. He saw that he was helping nobody, not even himself. He resolved to change his life, to break away from his rich, idle companions, and to draw closer to God and His poor. Instead of wasting his time in search of pleasure, he now began to visit the poor in their homes and in the hospitals and to spend many hours daily in the churches of Assisi.

### 3. THE DREAMER AND HIS DREAMS

About this time, St. Francis had a dream. A beautiful marble palace appeared before him, filled with arms of war. Shields, helmets, swords, and spears glistened from the polished walls, and upon each was emblazoned the sign of the cross. A voice, mild and clear, echoed in the palace, saying: "These are for you and your soldiers. Success will crown your efforts if you fight under my banner."

The dreamer was awakened early the next morning by the rays of the sun shining into his room. He blessed himself; then like a flash, he bounded from the bed and dressed. His prayers were said that morning with more piety than usual. With bowed head and clasped hands, he knelt before an old ivory crucifix. "Dear Lord," he prayed, "in all things great and small, it is my desire to please Thee. Teach me to act according to Thy will."

Francis wondered what the dream meant. "Perhaps God wants me to be a great soldier," he thought. A famous general with his army was at that time camping about a day's journey south of Assisi. The thoughts of the saint turned southward and he resolved to join the army.

Bidding farewell to his parents, he rode through the city gates. Uphill and downhill along narrow, dusty roads he went until he neared the camp. The darkness of night had fallen as the tired traveler dismounted under an olive tree. Pulling a blanket about him, he lay down to sleep.

That night another dream came to the wearied youth. Our Lord appeared to him and asked, "Francis, who can do more good for you, the master or the servant, the rich man or the poor man?"

"The master and the rich man," replied Francis.

"Then why do you leave me, the Master and Owner of countless riches, for a mere man with whom you can only share slavery and poverty?"

"O Lord," cried Francis, "what wilt Thou have me do?"

"Return to Assisi," said the Lord. "You did not

understand your dream.  I spoke to you of victories and of arms, but these are not the bloody battlefields of earth nor the shields and swords of steel.  You are to fight for the souls of men and your weapons will be prayer and penance.  Return to Assisi and await my message."

This dream was too real to be disregarded.  It seemed certain that God did not want him to enlist as a soldier.  For a time, the disappointment saddened him as he gazed at the tents of the army a short distance away.  His hopes of being a great general seemed shattered.

He gently patted the glossy neck of Nero, his spirited black horse; then, leaping into the saddle, he grasped the reins and turned the horse towards Assisi.  "Back home," he cried, spurring the beast onward.

## 4. THE MESSAGE

What excuse could he give his relatives and friends for his return?  He resolved to say nothing about his dream.  His parents were greatly surprised when they heard the clatter of the horse's hoofs on the cobblestones in the courtyard before their home.  His mother hurriedly withdrew the iron bolt from the door and folded her beloved son in her arms.

"Welcome!  A thousand welcomes!" she cried.  "I am so glad that you did not join the army but have returned to us."

Francis now spent more time than before in good works and prayer. He learned to love the poor and was never happier than when giving them money or food. He visited hospitals daily, and wherever he went, a ray of sunshine seemed to pass from him. No wound was too terrible for him to dress. The poor, suffering patients smiled in their pains as Francis, the son of the rich merchant, passed from cot to cot.

One warm afternoon, he was a little weary after visiting the sick and the poor. He wandered out through the city gates and down a shaded lane to the small wayside chapel of St. Damien, a stone church fast falling in ruins. The quietness of the place had always appealed to him, because he prayed more fervently when alone with God.

Ivy and moss had crept up the crumbling walls and hid the cracks. Cypress trees that never knew an owner's care towered high around the chapel and shaded it from the burning rays of the hot Italian sun. Pulling aside the heavy leather door, Francis entered the cool, damp church. The only sign of life was the tiny light that flickered in the red glass before the tabernacle.

The heart of the saint was filled with joy. Alone with God, he burst forth in prayer. "O Great God and Father of mercies," he prayed, "I adore Thee, I love Thee, I wish to serve Thee. Teach me, dear Lord, to do Thy holy will."

With tender affection, Francis raised his eyes to the large crucifix above the altar and recalled the bitter sufferings of his divine Master. Tears of sympathy rolled down his cheeks. Suddenly the thorn-crowned head seemed to turn. The saint was startled. Then a smile came from the cross. The lips moved, and Francis heard the words, "Francis, go and repair my church which you see falling into ruins."

The holy youth tried to answer but words would not come. In his heart, he said, "Dear Lord, I shall not rest until it is done."

## 5. FRANCIS STARTS HIS WORK

After some minutes, the happy young man rose from his prayers and sought the feeble old monk in charge of the chapel. He emptied his purse into the hands of the surprised priest, telling him that he would return soon with more money to pay for repairing the church.

Francis hastened back to the city and to the store of his father, Peter Bernadone. The shop was closed during the hot hours of the afternoon, as is even to-day the custom in that part of Italy.

With his key, Francis opened the shop and gathered together bolts of all sorts of silks, woolens, and linens. He loaded these on the back of a lively brown-black donkey, belonging to his family, which had been tied to a post near the shop. He led the beast to the market square of the town of Orvieto, some twelve miles distant. Both goods and donkey were sold at fair prices, for Francis was a clever salesman, especially when selling for the Lord.

His pockets filled with money and his heart filled with joy, he returned to St. Damien's and offered the priest the result of the day's sale. The good monk had never handled such a large sum of money before and became suspicious.

"Where did you get this money?" he demanded.

When Francis told the story, the priest was shocked. He scolded the well-meaning youth and refused to accept the money. Francis was offended and cast the money on a window sill in the church. Never for a moment did he think that he did wrong in selling his father's goods to help repair God's church.

"At least, Father," he begged, "you will let me stay here with you."

## 6. AN ANGRY FATHER AND HIS SON

When Peter Bernadone found out what his son had done, his anger knew no bounds. Few of his pennies had ever been given in charity and many a beggar had been turned away hungry from his door. The thought that his son had given a great deal of his money in charity was too much for the old merchant. Grasping a stout walking stick, he mounted his faithful horse and galloped toward St. Damien. His wife sent a messenger on ahead to warn Francis of his coming.

The church was empty when the enraged man entered. No prayer crossed his trembling lips as he looked around for his son, resolved to thrash him soundly with his cane. But Francis had fled to a cave. As Peter approached the altar, he saw a kind-faced monk with short, curly, grey locks falling about his ears and neck. Forgetting that he was in the house of God, Peter began to abuse the monk.

"Hold your tongue, my good man," said the priest. "You stand on holy ground. You have no reason for alarm. Your money remains untouched on yonder window sill. God has no use for tainted gold in His holy cause."

The old man grabbed the money and left the chapel without speaking further to the monk.

For many days, Francis remained in his cave, spending his days and nights in prayer and eating the food that his mother sent him by a servant. Finally, he decided to return to Assisi and meet his father. Dressed like a beggar in torn, ill-kept clothes, he walked through the streets of his native town. The children were surprised at his ragged appearance and thought that he must be crazy. They called him vile names, pelting stones and mud at him.

As the tattered youth entered his home, his father cursed in a rage and reached for his cane to beat him.

"Has it come to this?" he cried. "Must the proud Peter Bernadone go down to the grave disgraced by his crazy son? Out of my sight, you scoundrel! Out of my home forever!"

"But my good father," pleaded Francis, "I do not wish to offend you. I have never —"

"Silence, you wretch!" snarled the father. "You have gone too far now. To-morrow I shall take you before the bishop and you will be deprived of your right to be my heir. Not one penny of my wealth shall ever fall into your ungrateful hands."

"Father, I have learned that silver and gold are not the source of true happiness. I have no —"

"Out! Out!" shouted the merchant. "Get out before I strike you."

The next morning, father and son appeared before the bishop. Francis was wearing his best clothes, a satin tunic and mantle that he had not worn for a long time. The father in an angry voice denounced Francis to the bishop, declaring that he wished to deprive him of any share in his wealth.

The bishop turned to Francis and asked, "Have you any answer to make to these charges?"

Gently Francis answered, "I have nothing to say to them."

THE TRIAL BEFORE THE BISHOP

The bishop then proceeded to make out the papers required by law.

Francis removed his hat, tunic, and mantle, his shoes and stockings, and threw them on a pile in the middle of the floor. Then in a clear voice, he spoke to his father: "Thus far through life, I have called you father. Keep your money and take your clothes, because from now on I can truly say, 'Our Father Who art in heaven.'"

The father blushed with shame before the people and hurried to hide himself in his home.

## 7. The Church Is Repaired

St. Francis was soon back at St. Damien's, resolved more than ever to repair it. Begging in the streets was the plan by which he decided to get the money. When the poorly clad beggar appeared, many of his youthful companions recognized him. They laughed and jeered at their former friend and taunted him about his faith. At first this was hard to stand, but Francis humbled himself and patiently bore the ridicule. Money came slowly from the rich, but the peasants were glad to help him, bringing bricks and helping in the work of repairing. It was not long before the church was entirely repaired.

One task completed, Francis began another. He begged from door to door to repair the church of St.

Peter and the famous shrine called the Portiuncula.
It was at the latter place he made his home.　Here he
spent two years in prayer, preparing himself for the
great work that God had planned for him.

### 8. The Beginning of the Franciscans

During Mass one morning, the words of the gospel
struck Francis in a special manner: "Going forth,
preach.　Possess not gold nor silver, nor money in
your purse, nor two coats, nor shoes, nor a staff, for
the workman is worthy of his hire."　To fulfill this
command, Francis set aside his shoes, mantle, and
staff.　He made a tunic from coarse brown cloth and
tied it with a rope around his waist.　In this garb, he
began to preach to the people of Assisi and the neighboring towns.　They soon learned to love and admire
the humble and sincere friend of the poor.

His zeal and piety drew others to him and before
long a little community of holy men was gathered
under his direction.　Their days were passed in prayer,
in preaching, and in working.　No member was ever
permitted to accept money.　After a day's labor, they
were allowed to take only simple foodstuffs as pay and
this they had to bring to the monastery where all the
brothers lived.　Francis insisted on holy poverty in
everything.　The monks were forbidden to own anything.

It seems strange that a community with such strict rules should increase so rapidly. In ten years it had spread all over Italy and into parts of Switzerland, France, Germany, and Spain. When Francis called a meeting of all his followers about ten years after the community started, over five thousand answered the call. The followers of Francis were preaching the gospel of Jesus Christ in almost every country of Europe. This, then, was the fulfillment of Francis' dream. This was the army of which he was the captain. This was the army with weapons of prayer and penance.

As the years passed, Francis gradually withdrew as ruler and director of his community. The ruling of the order went into other hands, to give Francis more time to spend with God in prayer. He often wandered away to some lonely mountain cave to enjoy a silent hour or two with his Savior.

## 9. The Mark of God's Love

On one occasion, he climbed the heights of Mount Alvernia with a companion. Alone in a cave, he spent his days and nights in prayer, eating once a day the bread and water placed at the mouth of the cave by his companion. While praying one day, the cave suddenly brightened up and he saw an angel having the body of a man and with six large wings covering the body. Francis recognized the face of Christ. His heart was overflowing with love for Jesus Who loved him so much.

"My God and my All," he murmured over and over again.

As the vision disappeared, Francis became aware of sharp stinging pains in his hands, feet, and side. The pains became more intense and Francis felt something warm trickle down his side and over his hands and feet. He looked down and beheld blood running from deep wounds in his hands, feet, and side. These were representations of the five wounds on our Lord's body. It was a proof of the special love of God for His faithful servant.

## 10. THE END

Francis was brought back to his convent. His body was weakened by fasting and sickness, but for two years he lingered on, suffering in patience and waiting with joy the arrival of death, when he would join God in heaven. As the end drew near, he asked to be placed upon the ground with a tunic thrown over him. He did not wish to have a better deathbed than his Master.

"Farewell, my children," he said to his followers. "Remain always in the fear of the Lord. Happy will they be who continue in the good they have begun. I hasten to go to our Lord, to Whose grace I commend you."

His strength was gone. The lighted candle fell from his withered hands. With a sigh of relief, he passed to eternity.

### CHOOSE THE CORRECT WORD

In each sentence, only one of the words in parentheses is correct. Copy the sentences, choosing the word which completes each correctly.

1. Francis was (Italian, French, German).
2. He was (ugly, plain, handsome).
3. He was (dull, merry, serious).
4. As a youth, he wanted to be a (lawyer, doctor, soldier).
5. Francis was (brave, timid, cowardly).
6. He spent his youth in (study, pleasure, work).
7. Francis later learned to love the (rich, nobles, poor).
8. After his dreams, he spent a great deal of time in (schools, hospitals, theaters).
9. The father of Francis was (generous, gentle, selfish).
10. The (rich, nobles, poor) were glad to help Francis rebuild St. Damien's.

# SAINT HEDWIG

*(1174–1243)*

## 1. The New Convent

"For breaking the law of the land, I condemn you to work without pay for six months on the new convent at Trebnitz," said the Duke of Poland to four young men who were brought before him for robbery.

This was indeed a strange sentence. The robbers looked at one another in surprise. Some of their friends had been sentenced to gloomy dungeons and a bread-and-water diet. Others more wicked had been exiled from the country. But who ever heard of men being condemned to build a convent?

Hedwig, the pious wife of the duke, had urged her husband to build a large convent for the Sisters at Trebnitz. From her own funds she had given thousands and thousands of dollars and her friends were generous in helping the good work.

There was plenty of stone in the neighboring quarries and there were many mules to carry the stone to the place which had been chosen for the convent. But the skilled workers were few. The duke recalled the old Roman idea of forcing convicts to labor and he followed this plan to secure workmen for the building. The work, however, went along slowly, and it was several years before the convent was finished. When at last the Sisters moved in, the duchess was happy to think that another dwelling place had been erected for the honor and glory of God.

## 2. HER DAILY LIFE

Although St. Hedwig dwelt in a beautiful palace with a small army of servants to wait on her and with knights and ladies to honor her, she lived a life of poverty, fasting, and prayer. In her chamber the soft bed with its fancy satin coverlets was never disturbed. A plain cot thrown upon the floor was the bed she used. Except on state occasions, the duchess never wore the gorgeous robes of satin and ermine that became her position as the wife of the ruler of Poland. A simple dress hid the coarse hair shirt that she always used.

Her food was of the plainest kind. For forty years no meat ever entered her mouth. Every day, except Sunday, was a fast day for her. On Wednesdays and Fridays, her only food was bread and water. Thirteen poor ragged beggars were fed each day by Hedwig before she sat down to her own humble dinner.

Winter and summer, the holy duchess often walked several miles to church in her bare feet, carrying her shoes under her arm. At the sound of anyone approaching, she put on her shoes because she wished to keep her penances a secret between herself and God.

It was not unusual for Hedwig to spend days and nights in prayer. Long before the other members of the palace rose from their slumbers, St. Hedwig would quietly make her way to the chapel and greet her Lord in prayer. Alone in the breaking dawn, she silently adored her God.

When the sun appeared and sent its first beams through the colored glass windows, the great bronze bell in the tower called the household to Mass. As, one by one they tramped in, they always found the saintly mistress of the palace already in her place, her head bowed in prayer. Those who sat close by often saw tears of love drop from her eyes during the Holy Sacrifice — tears of love for the God Who bled and died at the great sacrifice of Calvary. Long after the altar boys had put out the candles, long after all others had left, the holy duchess continued her prayers.

Hedwig trained herself to be meek and humble like her heavenly Master. No angry or hasty word was ever known to cross her lips. Her way of correcting servants was so charming that no one was ever offended and yet those corrected never failed to follow the advice given. In fact, the servant who was so unfortunate as to need correction would grieve sincerely for having offended so lovable a mistress.

### 3. RESIGNED TO GOD'S WILL

St. Hedwig always finished her prayers with a request that God give her the grace of being resigned to His holy will. "O almighty and most merciful Lord," she would say, "teach me to see Thy holy will in all the trials that Thou may send upon me."

One day a messenger dashed into the courtyard on a steed covered with foam and sweat. He brought a report that the duke had been captured and was held prisoner at the castle of his bitter enemy.

On hearing of the misfortune of their master, the servants cried aloud. The family broke into tears at the news. Henry, the eldest son and heir, swore vengeance and resolved to lead an army against the enemy. The only person who held her peace and remained calm was the one most concerned, the beloved duchess. No words of rage escaped her lips. No tears of sorrow fell.

"Your father's capture, my dear children," she said without emotion, "has taken place according to the holy will of God. Let us be resigned. God knows best. However, I have every hope that we shall soon see your father at liberty and in good health."

"With my army I shall hasten that day!" exclaimed Henry.

St. Hedwig Demands Her Husband's Freedom

"I beseech you to hold your peace. There will be no need for shedding loyal Polish blood. I shall go to your father's captor and, with God's help, your father will dine with you before the set of Sunday's sun."

With a few attendants, she rode to the castle where her husband was a prisoner. The lord of the castle was a rough, surly man who never felt happy unless he had a sword dangling at his side. The Duchess Hedwig was ushered into the large reception hall where the master of the castle awaited her. She was so gracious and meek that the savage old warrior blushed with shame. Her request was made firmly yet gently, and the soldier could not help grant it.

A few years later, Hedwig's beloved husband died. Her friends came to offer sympathy on her loss. They were all surprised to find the duchess quite contented and resigned to the will of God.

"Would you complain against what God has done?" she asked one of her friends. "He is the master of our lives. We should train ourselves to wish what He wishes, whether that be our own death or the death of those near and dear to us."

## 4. In the Convent

After the death of the duke, Hedwig withdrew to the convent of Trebnitz which her husband had built at her request. Although she was the widow of the ruler of Poland and the builder of the convent, she would accept no privileges nor favors. In spite of her old age, she insisted on keeping the strict rule of the community, adding a few rules for herself to make it more severe. Her habit was a worn-out, cast-off dress that one of the other Sisters thought useless. Humbly she mingled with the nuns, making herself the least of them.

With the passing of years, St. Hedwig had another chance of showing how resigned she was to the will of God. Henry, her eldest son, was mortally wounded in a battle while fighting an army of savage barbarians who had attacked his kingdom. His wife was frantic with grief and hastened to Hedwig for consolation and sympathy.

The saint tenderly gathered the weeping widow to her breast and caressed her. "Weep not," she said softly. "It was the will of God that your noble husband should die fighting for his people. Blessed be His holy name!"

With her arm about her beloved daughter-in-law, she led her to the convent chapel. Both knelt before the great Comforter of the afflicted.

"Dear Lord," prayed the mother, "we give Thee thanks for having given us such a wonderful son and husband. To live with him during the past years was our greatest happiness. But now, we have a still greater happiness in seeing him united with Thee in Thy heavenly kingdom."

The example of the saintly mother had its effect on the poor heartbroken widow. Quietly she rose from her prayers, resigned to the will of God.

## 5. UNITED WITH GOD

The years of fasting and hardships had told upon the strength of St. Hedwig. Her remaining days were spent in prayer and in thinking of the passion of her divine Lord and Master. Long before her friends suspected that her end was near, she herself asked for the last sacraments. She was perfectly resigned to die at the time and in the manner chosen by God. Over and over again, she repeated the words of her Savior, "O Father, not my will but Thine be done." One evening the angel of death entered her cell and brought her home to God.

### CAN YOU

1. Give a better title to this story?
2. Tell two stories to show that St. Hedwig was resigned to God's will?
3. Tell how Hedwig spent her day in prayer?
4. Tell why she lived in such a humble, simple manner and performed such penances?
5. Tell how Hedwig lived at the convent?

# SAINT HYACINTH

*(1185–1257)*

## 1. The Sons of St. Dominic

"God speed you on your journey. Go back to your beloved Poland. Through the length and breadth of the land, urge the people to prayer and penance. Bring back the wandering souls to the fold of Jesus Christ. Visit the neglected people of the North and preach to them the gospel of the Savior. Carry nothing with you except the holy habit that you wear. Your heavenly Father will take care of your needs. Trust in God and be kind to the poor."

It was St. Dominic who was bidding farewell to a little band of Polish missioners who were returning to their fatherland. They had come to Rome on a visit as men of wealth and position, traveling in expensive coaches and waited on by servants. The wonderful works of St. Dominic and his white-robed monks so impressed them that they had joined his community and they were now returning to Poland as disciples and apostles of Him Who is called the Man of Poverty, traveling on foot and owning nothing but the plain white habit and the black mantle they wore. Gold and silver they had none, but God had given them a wealth of grace and a power to win the hearts of men — a treasure that no earthly gold could buy.

## 2. HOMEWARD BOUND

These zealous sons of St. Dominic, led by a monk named Hyacinth, journeyed on foot through the plains of central Italy, climbing the mountains in the north, then crossing Austria to their own country. The winding, stony mountain roads bruised and blistered their sandaled feet. They were drenched by torrents of rain. They were burned by the hot rays of the sun in the valleys and chilled by the frosts on the mountain tops. But on and on they cheerfully went, preaching here and there in some city or village.

God blessed all their efforts. People flocked in large numbers to hear the new preachers from Rome. So sincere and forceful were the sermons, that everywhere they stopped, the people begged them to remain longer among them. At times they remained long enough in a place to establish monasteries for the priests and pious laymen who joined their ranks.

The arrival of St. Hyacinth and his companions in Poland was the cause of great rejoicing among all classes of people. Stories of the wonderful success of the sons of St. Dominic had long before reached the country because the missioners had left a trail of glory from Rome to Poland. There was great demand in the kingdom for the services of the holy Dominicans.

The people seemed inspired with a new religious zeal. Sinners gave up their lives of crime. The lukewarm became more fervent. Men took a new interest in their churches and their faith.

As the years passed, men of all ranks became disciples of St. Hyacinth and joined the order of St. Dominic. Monastery after monastery was opened in the different parts of Poland and the white-robed fathers became the popular preachers of the country.

### 3. A PUBLIC MIRACLE

One year in the late spring, St. Hyacinth was invited to visit the Dominican monastery on the other side of the Vistula River. Warm spring weather had caused the snow and ice on the neighboring mountains to melt. Little torrents raced down the mountain sides and emptied themselves into the Vistula. Soon the river became a swift moving torrent, overflowing its banks and bringing destruction and ruin along its course.

When St. Hyacinth arrived at the river, the current was dashing so furiously that the boatmen refused to row across. The saint glanced at the other side and saw the hundreds of people who had gathered to hear him preach. He did not wish to disappoint them.

ST. HYACINTH WALKS ACROSS THE VISTULA RIVER

Making the sign of the cross over the river, he walked to the other side as if walking on dry land.

The people cheered and clapped when he reached the other shore. They flocked about him to kiss his hand or the sleeve of his habit. He needed to preach no sermon that day. The miracle was enough to give faith to the unbeliever and change the heart of the sinner.

## 4. THE WANDERING APOSTLE

With the heart of a true apostle, Hyacinth longed to bring other nations under the influence of the church of God. The pagan people to the north of Poland had resisted former efforts to Christianize them. St. Hyacinth resolved to take up the task again.

He climbed snowcapped mountains. He traveled miles and miles over fields of snow and ice as he went from city to city, preaching the word of God. Where others failed he succeeded. In order to be sure that his good work would last, Hyacinth established monasteries and trained priests to carry on what he had started.

Prussia, Russia, Denmark, Sweden, and Norway were visited by the great apostle. Thousands and thousands were converted and pledged themselves to spread the faith of Jesus Christ. Hyacinth's heart was happy at the success of his labors.

## 5. Among the Russians

Hyacinth spent many years in Russia where he built the famous monastery at Kiow, a city which was then the capital of the country. Here lived a people made up of pagans and bad Catholics. The work of converting them was not an easy task. The apostle, however, did not cease until he had brought back the fallen-away Catholics and converted many others.

One afternoon he was sauntering along the banks of the Nieber River when he noticed a throng of people on an island in the middle of the river. They were kneeling in adoration before a tree, worshiping it as a god. He was shocked and angered at the sight. He made the sign of the cross over the river and walked over it to the other side.

The pagans jumped to their feet when they saw the saint walking on the water. Hyacinth preached to them a wonderful sermon on the worship of the great God Who created heaven and earth and all things. He showed them how foolish it was to kneel down before a tree and worship it.

"Tear down the tree," he cried, "and worship the God Who made it." The eyes of the people were opened. They realized that he had come from God. The light of faith dawned upon them and they believed in the God about whom Hyacinth spoke.

## 6. THE CLOSING YEARS

Many years had passed since St. Hyacinth had left his native land to spread the gospel in the northern countries. A longing to return to his beloved Poland gave him no rest till he found himself back with his relatives and friends in the city of Cracow. Here the people, loyal and devout Catholics, were practicing the faith in a wonderful manner. This pleased the holy monk very much and, if he could have looked into the future, he would have been happy to see that, down through the centuries, the Polish people would continue to practice that faith in spite of sorrows and persecutions.

The apostolic spirit of Hyacinth would not let him rest when he thought there was work to do. After two years, he started out to visit all the monasteries he had established in Lithuania, Sweden, Norway, Denmark, and Russia. Then seeking new fields for his missionary labors, his footsteps led him across Russia and into the very heart of China.

The great Polish missionary was now seventy-two years of age. Old age had weakened him. He turned his tottering steps toward home. The holy apostle made a farewell speech to the members of his monastery and died, as he had foretold, on the feast of the Assumption.

1. When bidding farewell to his disciples, Dominic said: ——.
2. Instead of gold and silver the missioners had ——.
3. To get to Poland, the missioners had to cross ——.
4. On the arrival of St. Hyacinth in Poland, there was great rejoicing because ——.
5. Hyacinth performed the miracle at the Vistula River because ——.
6. The countries in which Hyacinth preached were ——.
7. He worked a miracle in Russia because ——.
8. During the last years of his life he visited ——.

# SAINT LOUIS, KING OF FRANCE

*(1215–1270)*

## 1. The Little Prince

A gentle evening breeze from the royal gardens caused the tiny flames of the candles to flicker and cast strange figures in lights and shadows on the gilded ceiling. Queen Blanche was resting in her favorite armchair. Lying at her feet, with his arm around his pet collie dog, was her young son, Prince Louis. He was gazing at the shadows dancing above him. The drowsy boy was tired of his books and toys, which were scattered over the floor. He was about to fall asleep.

The bell in the chapel tower slowly tolled the hour, and the sound roused the queen from her dreams.

"You are tired, Louis," she said. "Kneel beside me and say your prayers and then trip off to bed."

The prince ran his little fingers through the long brown silken hair of his dog and went to kneel at the side of the queen. With his hands clasped together, he piously recited the prayers his mother had taught him. His last prayer was always the same, "O dear Lord, I never want to offend you; so keep me free from sin."

After blessing himself, he arose and threw his arms around his mother's neck. She kissed the upturned face and said: "My son, you must never forget that last prayer. Sin is the only great evil in the world. Louis dear, you know how much I love you. No mother could love her son more than I love you. But I would sooner see you lying dead at my feet than know that you had offended your God by one mortal sin."

"Mother," replied the little prince, "you know that I have promised our Lord that I shall never commit a mortal sin and I shall keep that promise till the day I die."

Another good-night kiss and the boy was off to bed.

Louis had heard his mother speak like that often before. He was but a child of ten, still he knew that a mortal sin must be something terrible in God's sight or his mother would not have such a horror of it. As he grew older, those words of his beloved mother remained in his mind. Even as a soldier-king on the battlefield, he had them always before him. That warning kept him free from mortal sin and made him one of the great heroes of God's church.

## 2. A Troublesome Kingdom

When Louis was twelve years old, his father died. Thus as a mere boy he was crowned king of France, but his mother ruled the kingdom until he became of age.

It was no easy task to govern France in those troublesome days. Many of the noble and powerful men of the kingdom plotted the overthrow of the boy-king. Armies were raised in rebellion. The news reached the royal palace but did not frighten the queen. Like a brave general, she ordered her troops into the field and led them against Count Theobald, the most powerful of the warring nobles.

The faithful soldiers of France fought bravely under their courageous queen and soon brought the rebellious count to his knees. The defeat of the leader caused the others to tremble and before long they all knelt before the young king and promised to be loyal.

Twice the king of England with a small army entered France and challenged Louis. The young king gathered his loyal forces together and sallied forth and drove the enemy across the channel to England. The nobles at home and the enemy abroad soon learned that King Louis could hold his own on the battlefield and that to oppose him meant defeat. Thus peace was brought to his kingdom.

The king now turned his mind toward the welfare of his people. For years and years, they had suffered under unjust laws. St. Louis changed these laws and thus helped the common people. To the sick and poor he was very kind. Food and money were sent in abundance from the royal palace for them. Hospitals, schools, and churches were built for them. The people of France saw the wonderful things done by the king and they came to love him as few kings have ever been loved.

In his own daily life, the king was a model of virtue and piety. A certain part of each day was set aside for prayer and he always began the day by hearing the holy sacrifice of the Mass in the royal chapel. At the dinner table, he always deprived himself of certain delicious foods as a penance. Improper or coarse language was forbidden in the royal presence. Those who dared to talk about the vulgar or the impure were banished from court, and severe punishment was given to those who misused the Holy Name.

## 3. A CRUSADER'S VOW

From time to time, sad stories reached France about the sufferings of the Christians in the Holy Land, the place where Jesus lived and died. The Mohammedans cruelly persecuted the Christians and inflicted all sorts of torture on them. For years the cry throughout Europe had been, "Let us rescue the Holy Land from the Turks." Several unsuccessful attempts had already been made. These wars were called *crusades* and those who took part in them were called *crusaders*.

King Louis pitied the poor sufferers and often sent shiploads of food and large sums of money to the Christians. The thought of leading an army to the Holy Land had come to the mind of the saintly king more than once, but he had so much to take care of at home that he had found it impossible.

Once, however, being stricken with a serious illness, he hung between life and death for several days. One afternoon, the doctors and attendants thought that the end had come. But quite suddenly, Louis rose from his supposed deathbed and cried out that he wanted to take the vow of a crusader. His mother and wife hurried into the darkened room and tried to calm him, thinking that the fever had affected his mind. The king grew angry and insisted that the bishop of Paris be called to give him the cross of a crusader and to accept his vow to go to the Holy Land.

Excited and nervous, the bishop entered the sickroom. "Give me the cross of the crusader and accept my vow," demanded the king.

"Your Majesty, you are too weak to think about such things," said the bishop. "Wait till you get stronger."

But for Louis there was to be no waiting. "No food nor drink," he said, "will cross my lips until my vow is made."

When the bishop saw that Louis would not change his mind, he placed upon the king's shoulders the red cross of the crusader. The king knelt beside the bed and took a vow that he would go to the Holy Land to save the places made sacred by the life of our Lord.

### 4. OFF FOR THE HOLY LAND

Preparations began almost immediately after the king's recovery. He announced to the people of France that he intended to lead an army to drive the Turks from the Holy Land and asked for volunteers. Wild enthusiasm spread rapidly over the country and the bravest and fairest of the soldiers of France pledged themselves to follow their king. The shipyards hummed with life, as new boats were built and old ones repaired. In about two years all things were ready.

Unfurling the banner of France, St. Louis, accompanied by some of his knights, rode into the port from which they were to set sail. Thousands of heroes awaited their leader. Thunderous applause greeted the happy monarch as he arrived at the camp on his black horse spattered with dust and foam. "Hail to the ruler of France! Long live the king! Down with the infidel!" shouted the soldiers on all sides. Louis was truly proud of that vast army of loyal hearts that was going forth from home and country to fight for the land of Jesus.

Orders were given to board the ships. One hundred

and twenty-eight large vessels and about one thousand small ones were floating at anchor in the harbor. Brawny-armed sailors rowed the boats to the shallow beach. Before long, sixty thousand soldiers and one thousand knights had climbed aboard.

There was silence for a minute while the priests asked for the blessing of God on the journey. Then from every boat voices broke forth in a hymn in honor of Mary, the Star of the Sea. The heavy anchors were hauled in and the boats sailed away toward the Isle of Cyprus.

## 5. FACING THE ENEMY

The expedition remained at the Isle of Cyprus for several months, waiting for more soldiers from England and a favorable time to strike the enemy. It was decided to attack the Turks at their strongest forts. The cities of Damietta and Cairo in Egypt were to be taken first, and with these strongholds in their power, the Christians thought that they could easily march through the land in victory.

It was a gala day at Cyprus, with cannons booming, church bells ringing, and flags waving as the Christian fleet set out for Egypt. Four days of sailing brought the boats before the fortified city of Damietta, at the mouth of the Nile River. The enemy had already seen the invaders. The sultan brought his fleet to the mouth of the river to prevent the Christian ships from sailing up the Nile. Brown-skinned Turkish soldiers were stationed along the shore. They jeered at the approaching Christians and brandished their shining scimitars in the air.

"Death to the Christian dog," they cried. "Death to the invader."

Their savage taunts and threats only spurred on the soldiers of France. The king commanded the ships to be brought as far up on the sandy beach as possible. With sword in hand, he was the first to leap into the shallow waters.

"Forward, brave heroes of France," he cried. "Follow your king. Whether we conquer or die, we shall glorify God, either by the success of our arms or by the shedding of our blood. Onward to victory!"

The soldiers in the boats nearest the land quickly jumped into the water and followed Louis. Holding their shields to their breasts and with their long sharp lances thrust before them, they formed a wall along the shore to prevent the Turks from assaulting the others as they landed.

Again and again, the Turkish cavalry galloped at the Christian lines, but each time they were driven back by deadly blows from the French and English lances. The Christian lines remained unbroken until the last soldier landed.

St. Louis before the Walls of Damietta

The hearts of the enemy trembled as Louis' army advanced on the city of Damietta. The sultan's forces were routed at every attack. Seeing no hope of saving the beautiful city, the angry Turks set fire to it and fled. The quick action of the Christians saved the city from flames.

The king and his staff with the bishops and priests who were with the expedition marched to the largest church in the city and blessed it in honor of Mary, the Mother of God. Kneeling in prayer, they humbly thanked God for their first great victory. Louis immediately forbade the soldiers to plunder the town or to injure the peaceful inhabitants.

## 6. FIGHTING AT THE NILE

The Christians waited in Damietta for some months before they began their march toward Cairo. They were halted at a branch of the Nile River and, much to their surprise, beheld the enemy encamped on the other side. The French officers were puzzled. It would mean death to cross the river on rafts or in small boats as long as the Turks occupied the opposite bank. To build bridges would be impossible. Various schemes were tried but found useless.

The enemy was always on the alert. They terrified the Christians by hurling into the camp great balls of fire that destroyed tents and provisions and even killed soldiers.  Louis' followers had never seen such strange fire and found it impossible to put out the flames.

For three weary months, both armies watched each other, with the river quietly flowing between them. At length, a Turkish traitor for a sum of money showed the French a place where the river could be crossed in safety.  The entire army gained the other shore without a mishap.

An immediate assault was made on the Turkish camp. The three months of idle waiting had made the French desperate.  They dashed at the Turks with fierceness and determination and the enemy retreated in disorder.

The Christians followed in close pursuit, although some of the officers opposed the plan.

The fleeing infidels sought shelter within the walls of a neighboring stronghold.  At their heels ran the advance wing of the French army.  Brandishing their swords and lances, they followed the Turks within the gates of the city.  But alas! it was a fatal mistake.

The retreat of the enemy had been a mere trick to lure the French to death.  As soon as the last Christian entered the city, the gates were closed by the natives and every French soldier except two was put to death. This sad turn of events taught the French that they must be on their guard.

Battles followed in quick succession.  The Christians were lucky to hold their own.  The tide had turned in favor of the enemy. Louis saw that it was impossible to advance. He ordered a retreat to Damietta.

## 7. DEFEATED

The infidels attacked the retreating forces all along the march. The disheartened Christians began to suffer from the climate and soon sickness spread among them. This blow was more serious than the attacks of the enemy. The king was forced to halt the retreat and pitch camp. The crafty Turks were waiting for this chance. They quickly surrounded the Christians and forced them to surrender.

After terms were settled, the king and his army were set free for a large sum of money and the return of the city of Damietta. A truce was signed for ten years.

St. Louis, broken in health and saddened in spirits, visited the Holy Land before his return to France. It was here that he received word of the death of his beloved mother. Louis was bitterly grieved. Kneeling in his chapel, he prayed: "O God of mercies, You have taken from me the best of mothers. I loved her above all creatures of earth. I thank Thee for having given her to me for so many years. May Thy holy will be done." But the king's love for his mother did not end when she was placed in the grave. Ever afterwards, he had a Mass celebrated each day for the repose of her soul and he was always present to pray for the mother who was so dear to him.

With the remnants of his defeated army, King Louis soon sailed for home. He was not the same Louis that had left his kingdom six years before. The terrible sufferings and hardships of the war had left their marks upon him. He decided to spend the remaining years of his life in working for the welfare of his people. In his daily life, he imitated the poverty and piety of the monks. The poor and the sick were always the object of his tender sympathy. He visited them in the hospitals and sent them food and medicine. A word of kindness was ever on his lips for the afflicted and the downtrodden.

## 8. His Last Crusade

Over twenty years had now passed since Louis' return from Egypt. Through the length and breadth of his kingdom, he was known as the saintly king. Cries for help again reached his ears from the suffering Christians in the Holy Land. Those cries he could not resist. Although weakened by the trials of life and the burdens of age, he departed on another crusade.

The army landed at Carthage on the coast of Africa. The king fell ill. Knowing that his end was near, he sent for his eldest son and heir. The dying man from the fullness of his saintly heart bade farewell to his son and then spoke thus to him: "My son, above all things I recommend to you that you love God. Be ready to suffer all torments rather than commit a mortal sin. Be kind and generous to the poor. Shun evil companions. Never permit anyone to say anything sinful in your presence. In dealing with your subjects, be just and upright. After my death, have a great many Masses said for the repose of my soul. I bless you with the tenderest affection that a father can have for a son, and I pray that God will strengthen and protect you in His service."

The saintly old man lingered for some hours and finally died with these words on his lips, "O God, into Thy hands I commend my spirit."

### FIND THE PROOF

Find the sentence or sentences that prove each of the following statements to be right or wrong. Then number a paper from 1 to 10. After each number, write *Yes* if you have proved that the statement to which the number corresponds is true; write *No* if you have proved the statement false.

1. Queen Blanche hated mortal sin.
2. Louis promised never to commit a mortal sin.
3. All the nobles loved the boy-king.
4. Blanche was a cowardly queen.
5. St. Louis loved the poor.
6. The daily life of Louis was marked with piety.
7. The first crusade was small.
8. Louis knew how to encourage his soldiers in battle.
9. Louis forgot the memory of his mother after her death.
10. On his deathbed, St. Louis advised his son to be good.

# SAINT GERTRUDE

## (1221–1292)

### 1. A GIFT TO GOD

The rusty iron bell at the convent gate tinkled several times. The clatter of the portress's sandals was soon heard as the feeble old nun hurried over the flagstones to answer the call. Cautiously, she pulled the slide from a tiny window and peeped out to see who had rung. A sweet smile brightened her wrinkled face as she said, "Just a moment." She lost no time in drawing back the heavy bars and opening the gate. Gertrude, a timid little girl, five years of age, bashfully stepped inside.

Her pious parents, desirous of pleasing God, had brought her to the convent and offered her as a gift to the Lord. How dearly they must have loved God to consecrate to Him their charming little daughter! Do you remember the story of the boy Samuel whose mother gave him to God? These good parents knew that no greater honor could come to them than the honor of having their children serve the Lord of heaven and earth.

The Sisters loved God's little child. She was so

gentle, sweet, and kind that they could not help loving
her. Carefully they guided her young life in the ways
of knowing, loving, and serving God. Joy filled their
hearts as she grew in wisdom and piety from day to
day. The only fault for which they had to scold her
was her habit of leaving the children when at play to
hide in the convent chapel and pray.

## 2. St. Gertrude Becomes a Nun

Years passed, and St. Gertrude arrived at an age
when she was able to make a choice of vocation. The
holy life of the Benedictine Sisters with whom she lived
appealed to her. She asked to become a member of
their community. The Sisters were delighted to welcome their pious friend as a Sister in their convent.
They all knew that she had found favor in God's sight,
and they felt that she would bring God's blessing upon
them.

Now that St. Gertrude had consecrated herself
wholly to God, she lived in closer union with Him.
As often as possible, she knelt before His tabernacle
in the chapel and spoke to Him with the love and confidence of a child speaking to its earthly father.

## 3. St. Gertrude's Confidence in God

Indeed, she spoke to God about everything. There
was nothing in her life about which she did not consult

ST. GERTRUDE FINDS HER NEEDLE

Him, because she felt that He was interested in all that she did. Her confidence in the Lord was so strong that she was sure He would help her in everything that concerned her, no matter how small or how great it might be.

In the story of her life, we read that one day she lost a needle in a pile of straw. She saw the tiny piece of steel disappear beneath the thousands of blades of yellow grass and realized that it would be almost impossible to find it. She thought at once of her heavenly Friend. Closing her eyes, she prayed: "O dear Jesus, it would be wasting a great deal of time for me to look for my needle. Please get it for me." She confidently reached forth her hand and her fingers immediately closed over the needle.

It was to this wonderful confidence in God that St. Gertrude owed all the gifts she received from heaven. She knew that the Sacred Heart of Jesus was glad to be kind and generous to those who trust in Him.

4. St. Gertrude and the Blessed Sacrament

Gertrude's greatest joy was to receive her Lord in Holy Communion. That was the happiest moment of the day. She knew that beneath the appearance of the tiny white Host was the great God Whom she loved and adored, the God Who made the sky, land,

and sea. She knew that in Holy Communion she received the same God Who died on Calvary to save us.

St. Gertrude did all in her power to make her soul a fitting place to receive Him. Hers was no short, idle preparation, no hasty, thoughtless prayers. Her time for preparation never seemed long enough. With tears of sorrow she begged God's pardon for all the faults of her life. This was no mere prayer of the lips, but a sincere prayer that came from a heart crushed with anguish because it had offended the Redeemer of the world. Then words of tender love brushed away the tears of sorrow, words that told God that He was dearer to her than all the things of earth, words praying that His heart and hers would be joined together in time and eternity. She wished to have no desire in life except to please Him.

"O most sweet and loving Jesus," she prayed, "behold the longed-for moment draws near in which I shall receive the holy sacrament of Thy Body and Blood as a remedy for all my miseries. For the love of Thee, I grieve for all my sins by which I have offended Thy goodness and stained my soul. O how shall I dare to receive Thee into my worldly heart! Good Jesus, Thy invitation gives me confidence. I shall draw near to the sacred feast of the altar with a humble heart, with hope in Thy mercy and goodness, with love for

Thee and Thine, with an ardent desire to do Thy holy will as long as life lasts."

But these pious preparations seemed not to satisfy St. Gertrude. The thought of her unworthiness to be joined with her God always came before her mind. Here again, her confidence in God came to her rescue. "What good will it do to doubt and hesitate?" she asked. "Even in a thousand years I could not prepare myself worthily. In love, confidence and humility, I shall approach my God and He will make me worthy."

> O Lord I am not worthy
> That Thou shouldst come to me.
> But say the word of comfort
> And my spirit healed shall be.

How do we prepare ourselves to welcome our Lord in Holy Communion? Are our prayers short and hasty? Do we really mean what we say when we speak to God in our prayers? Perhaps we need to learn the lesson taught by the life of St. Gertrude.

### STUDY HELPS

1. How did St. Gertrude come to live at the convent?
2. Tell the story of Samuel and his mother.
3. Why did the Sisters love St. Gertrude?
4. What is meant by Gertrude's confidence in God?
5. Give two examples of this confidence.
6. Tell how Gertrude prepared for Holy Communion.
7. How do you prepare to receive our Lord?

# SAINT JOHN NEPOMUCENE

## (1330–1383)

## 1. THE WONDERFUL CURE

It was a grief-stricken mother who opened the door of her cottage for the parish priest. "Oh, Father," she cried, "I am so glad you have come. Baby John has been so sick that the doctor thinks that there is little hope for him. Pray for him, please, that God may cure him. I promise to give him back to serve the Lord all the days of his life."

The tender heart of the pastor was moved by the tears of his friend. He spoke a kind word to her, telling her that God would answer her prayers.

Quietly he entered the sickroom where, by the light of a candle, he saw the little babe rolling and tossing restlessly. The parents knelt beside the bed as the priest sprinkled the child with holy water.

"O God," the good priest prayed, "upon Whom we all depend for health and strength in youth and in old age, stretch forth Thy hand upon this little child that, being restored in health, he may live to a ripe old age and never fail to thank Thee and serve Thee faithfully. Through Jesus Christ Our Lord."

The parents devoutly answered, "Amen."

"O Father of mercies and God of all consolation," the priest continued, "Who dost provide for Thy creatures in loving kindness, healing them in body as well as in soul, be pleased to raise this little babe from its sickbed and restore him to Thy holy Church and to his parents, so that in the years that are to come he may serve Thee with a grateful heart."

Then stooping over the moaning child, he placed his right hand gently upon the fevered head. "They shall lay their hands upon the sick," he continued, "and they shall recover. May Jesus, the Son of Mary, the Lord and Protector of the world, show thee favor and mercy through the merits and prayers of His holy saints."

The mother wiped away her tears as she answered "Amen." A burden seemed lifted from her heart. She handed the priest a bottle of holy water. He sprinkled the sick child and blessed him with the sign of the cross, "May the blessing of Almighty God, the Father, Son, and Holy Ghost, descend upon you and remain with you forever. Amen."

When the doctor called the next morning, he was surprised to see his little patient sitting up in bed, playing with his toys. "This is, without doubt, a miracle," he exclaimed. "God must have some great work for this child to do, or He would not have given him back to you in this wonderful manner."

## 2. THE YOUNG PREACHER

After studying at the University of Prague, John was ordained to the holy priesthood. His fame as a speaker caused the bishop to give him charge of a parish near the university. The enthusiastic sermons of the young pastor soon became the talk of the city. With all the power of his soul, he fearlessly denounced vice and sin and called upon the students to reform their lives, to give up their drinking, gambling, and wickedness. The hearts of many were struck and they wept bitter tears of repentance.

One day a courier from King Wenceslas brought an invitation to Father John to preach during Lent in the chapel of the royal palace. The young priest smiled as he read the letter. It seemed to him strange that a king so wicked as the youthful ruler of Bohemia should ask him to preach at the castle.

There was no secret about the sinful life of the young king. John knew that it would be a difficult task to denounce sin and threaten the punishment of hell before Wenceslas. He felt, however, that there might be a faint chance of converting the king and his evil friends, and hence he accepted the invitation.

His sermons were far more successful than he had expected. Like another John the Baptist, he denounced every form of sin that made the royal court a scandal in the country. The grace of God worked with him and touched the hearts of those who listened. Old nobles hardened in sin and careless youths, whose lives gave promise of continuing the wickedness they saw on every side, and even the king himself praised the sermons and promised the saint that they would give up their vices.

The young priest made a great impression upon the king. Wenceslas tried to force him to be a bishop. St. John firmly refused. Later he offered him the position of lord chancellor of the kingdom, but this, too, Father John would not accept. He sought neither honors nor wealth. His whole soul was bent on saving sinners.

### 3. Court Confessor and Almoner

However, some time afterwards, John accepted the position of chief almoner or chaplain of the court. Here he saw a chance to reform the court by his sermons, because he was to make his home at the palace. But what pleased him most was the fact that he became the official friend of the poor and had charge of all the money to be given in charity. The sick and the poor never had any difficulty in reaching the heart of their friend and helper.

The Empress Jane, a noble, pious queen, admired the zeal and kindness of the court almoner. She urged him to continue his efforts to reform the court. From time to time, she, with many of the other members of the court, went to confession to St. John and sought his help and advice.

King Wenceslas loved his wife so dearly that he became jealous if any of the nobles spoke to her. This jealousy tormented him constantly. An evil suspicion of his queen haunted him night and day. He feared that she loved someone else.

Wenceslas spoke to a trusted companion about his suspicions. "You can easily find out whether she is a faithful wife," said his friend. "Call in Father John, her confessor, and ask him what the queen tells him in confession."

"But," protested the king, "a priest cannot make known to anyone what he hears in confession."

"You are king," answered his friend. "Command and he will obey."

King Wenceslas dispatched a messenger for the almoner of the court. Father John shortly appeared in the royal presence and was greeted cordially by the king.

The crafty ruler was too clever to make his demand outright. He began by asking questions to settle his own troubled conscience. St. John thought it strange that he was getting so pious.

Wenceslas then told of his worries about the health

of the queen. He gradually hinted that perhaps she was not happy. The almoner was surprised at this undue anxiety of the king and assured him that Queen Jane seemed well and happy.

Then Wenceslas grew impatient. His plan was working too slowly. He changed his manner and said sharply to St. John: "You are the confessor of the queen. I, King Wenceslas, have a right to know what my wife is thinking and doing. I demand that you tell me what she confesses to you."

The saint was dazed at this bold request. His face turned pale. His lips tightened about his mouth. He looked defiantly at the king and answered: "Your Majesty steps beyond your bounds. Your scepter commands the bodies of men but can never reach their souls. The seal that guards God's sacred confessional cannot be broken by the power of any king. I refuse to fulfill your request."

The face of Wenceslas flushed with anger. No one had ever dared to defy him before. "My word is law throughout this empire. My servants must obey my wishes. Answer my request or you will regret it for the rest of your life. I have dungeons and punishments for those who refuse to obey."

"Sir king," replied the almoner, "you have no dungeon dark enough and no punishment painful enough to make me break my vow to God. You may torture me; you may bury me in your filthy dungeons; you may even murder me, but I shall never break the seal of the confessional. On those things which the priest hears in that sacred tribunal his lips are sealed forever."

The king saw that to proceed further would be useless. He cast a look of disgust at the royal almoner and left the room. St. John understood the character of the stubborn king well enough to know that Wenceslas was not yet finished with him.

### 4. AT THE KING'S DINNER

Wenceslas avoided meeting the priest for some time after this angry scene. He sought the advice of those about the court who hated St. John for denouncing their wicked lives. They were somewhat afraid of the popularity of the saint and urged the king to wait for a chance to imprison him.

The occasion presented itself long before they expected it. One day Wenceslas was entertaining his friends at dinner. A chicken was served. When the king plunged the carving knife into its breast, he found that it was not cooked enough. Filled with anger, he flung the fowl at the head of the servant who had placed it on the table.

"Must I be insulted before my guests?" he yelled. "The cook will pay for this." Then turning to one of the soldiers who stood at attention in the dining hall, he said, "Tell the captain of the royal guard to roast the cook alive on the fire on which he should have roasted the chicken." Some of the heartless nobles laughed to encourage the savage king. Others turned pale but dared not protest.

The captain of the palace guard proceeded to obey the brutal command. The poor cook screamed and struggled in terror as the soldiers prepared to roast him alive. The other servants fled from the palace in fear. One of them met St. John and told of the cruel king's order.

The saint lost no time in hastening to the palace. He entered the banquet hall where the king and his drunken guests were making merry. He pleaded with the king to forgive the poor cook and spare his life. Wenceslas laughed at him. The more John pleaded, the more angry the king grew.

As a last resort, John cried out raising his hand to heaven: "Sir king, there is a just God who reigns on high. He will deal with you as you have dealt with others."

This threat was too much for the king. "Cast this vile wretch into prison," he said to the soldiers. "There in filth and hunger let him learn that he cannot insult the king of Bohemia. I hold in my hand the life and death of all my subjects."

## 5. The Saint Remains Firm

For several days John was kept in prison. The king pretended that he was being punished for publicly insulting His Majesty. John, however, knew the real reason. It was because he had refused to break the seal of the confessional.

At different times, the king sent messengers to him, offering him liberty on the condition that he reveal what the queen had told him in confession. But the prisoner remained true to the vow of his priesthood.

Finally a courier arrived at the prison with an order commanding the jail keeper to set Father John free. He also brought a warm invitation from the king to his almoner, begging his forgiveness and asking him to dine that evening at the royal palace.

John did not wish to offend the king without reason and accepted the invitation. Wenceslas was very gracious that night and publicly asked the pardon of St. John. After the other guests had left, the king began a private conversation with his almoner. He gradually led up to the question of the queen's confessions. Promises of secrecy and offers of power and wealth came one after another from the lips of the wicked ruler.

But to all his pleadings, the holy priest always gave the same answer, "I will never betray my trust."

Seeing that promises of reward could gain nothing, Wenceslas turned to threats. "You have already tasted my dungeons," he hissed through his teeth. "That is only a beginning of what I shall do unless you break your silence. My trusted soldiers will tie you to the rack and pull your limbs from their joints. This failing, they will apply torches to your body and roast you until you cry for mercy. But no mercy will be shown you till you obey your king."

"I laugh at your threats," replied the saint. "I scorn your tortures. Your soldiers may tear me limb from limb. They may roast me alive as the Romans roasted St. Lawrence. But no word will ever cross my lips about those things told me in the sacred tribunal of confession."

The almoner was now cast into prison and tortured as the king had threatened. During the severe pain, his lips were sealed and no words came from them except the names Jesus and Mary.

When Queen Jane heard of the sad plight of St. John, she hurried to the king and begged him to free the holy man. Wenceslas yielded to her entreaties and once more Father John returned to the palace.

In a vision, God told him that his days were numbered. With increased zeal, he preached of sin and its punishment. He pictured the sad end of those who lead wicked lives and urged the people to serve the

Lord with their whole heart and soul. The poor and the sick were tended with greater care than usual by the saint who walked in the shadow of death.

### 6. The Last Attempt

One evening Father John was returning to the royal palace after visiting the sick in a near-by village. Wenceslas sat at his window gazing into a cloudy sky. He noticed the familiar form trudging along the road with his empty basket in his hand. He sent a messenger to bring St. John to him.

With shoes and cassock covered with dust, the almoner entered the room. A few candles burned on the table near which the king sat. He motioned to St. John to take a seat before the open fireplace.

Without any further delay, the jealous king began: "I have stood enough of your nonsense. To-night you have your last chance. Either tell me what you have heard from the queen in the confessional or die the death."

"I prefer to die," answered the saint in a calm low voice.

"And die you will, you ungrateful wretch," cried the furious tyrant. "Soldiers! Guards!" he called loudly, pounding on the table with the hilt of his sword.

Several soldiers with drawn swords rushed into the room, thinking that someone was attacking the king.

"Bind this wretch hand and foot and cast him into the river at a place where the people will not see him. Do not return till you see his lifeless body sink for the last time."

## 7. THE MARTYR

The command was obeyed. The saint, bound and gagged, was hurled from the bridge into the slow-flowing stream. The brutal soldiers watched the body rise for the third time and then sink forever. They knew that their victim was dead and returned with the news to the king.

But God caused the body to float on the top of the River Muldow. Over it appeared golden lights that caused people to flock to the banks of the river. The queen noticed the lights from her window and sent messengers to the king to inquire about them. Wenceslas gave one glance toward the river and, beholding the lights, turned pale with fear. He hastened to a secret place and forbade anyone to follow him.

The next morning the whole town was astir with the story of the martyrdom of St. John. The people loved their friend and protector. As the body was brought in to shore, they gathered about, telling stories of his kindness to the poor and the sick. The corpse was carried in triumph through the streets, followed by men, women, and children who denounced the wicked Wenceslas.

St. John's Body Floating on the River

In the cathedral of Prague they laid the saint to rest. Over his tomb was placed a slab of marble with these words carved on it:

Under this stone, lies the body of St. John Nepomucene,
Who because he faithfully kept the seal of the confessional
Was cruelly tormented and thrown into the river
By order of Wenceslas, king of Bohemia.

Over three hundred years later, the tomb was opened. The body of the saint had turned to dust, but the tongue had remained just as it was in life.   It was God's way of showing His love for the martyr of the seal of His sacrament.

CAN YOU ANSWER THESE?

1.   What kind of sermons did St. John preach?
2.   What does *the seal of the confessional* mean?
3.   Why did John accept the king's invitation?
4.   Read the part of the story that shows that John was not ambitious.
5.   Why did John accept the position as almoner?
6.   What bold demand did the king make of St. John?
7.   Why was John dazed at this demand?
8.   Read the answer of St. John.
9.   Read the answer he gave after the king threatened him.
10.   Why is St. John called a martyr?

# JOAN OF ARC — THE SAVIOR OF FRANCE

*(1412-1431)*

## 1. JOAN AT HOME IN DOMRÉMY

At the beginning of the fifteenth century, in the little French village of Domrémy, lived Joan of Arc. In those days there was no school in the town, so Joan grew up without learning how to read or write. The good parish priest and her mother taught her about God and His holy Church and how to pray to Him. Joan's mother was a practical woman who wanted the girl to be skilled in all household duties. Therefore she learned to spin, sew, and cook. She often helped her brothers on the farm and was proud to show her strength. After sundown she could frequently be seen with her sheep dog, rounding up the cattle and driving them home to the barns.

She loved the birds, the flowers, the forest, the brook. In fact, she loved everything that God had made. When her work was done, she liked to roam through the neighboring woods, watching the birds and listening to their vesper songs. Time and again, in the soft twilight, St. Joan would wander along the winding forest paths with her rosary in her hand. Far removed from the eyes of men, this pious maiden would fall upon her knees beneath the leafy trees and speak lovingly to her God.

Her steps often brought her to the chapel where the tiny, flickering light reminded her of her Lord. Oh, how her soul thrilled with love and hope as she knelt in prayer before her God! All the joys and sorrows of her life were told to her Friend on the altar. Was it any wonder, then, that God should select this pure, simple maiden to do His work on earth?

## 2. MESSENGERS FROM HEAVEN

For several years Our Lord had been preparing Joan for a difficult task — the task of driving the enemies of her country from the land of France and of bringing her king to the city of Rheims for his coronation. Then from the glorious heights of heaven, God sent His messenger, the archangel Michael, to Joan when she was but thirteen years of age. The holy child was frightened at the dazzling light and the whispered message, "Be good and pious, my child, and go often to church." At the time, she did not know that it was the great archangel that spoke to her.

Again and again, that heavenly voice sounded in Joan's ears and told her of her mission. What a mission! This simple sturdy peasant girl was to be the savior of her country. This gentle maid was to lead the armies of France to victory.

As time went by, two other saints, St. Catherine and St. Margaret, appeared with St. Michael. Both wore glittering crowns of gold and spoke with soft musical voices. They told the shepherdess about the sad state of France. They pictured for her battle-fields soaked with the blood of French soldiers. Many of the fairest cities of France had been conquered by her enemies. The whole country seemed on the brink of doom. Each day, the uncrowned king, in fear and trembling, awaited the sad news that his beloved France was lost.

The voices told Joan that she was to be the savior of France. The very thought of it filled her heart with fear and terror. She knew that there were many others more capable and worthy of the task — great generals whose names were held in reverence at every French fireside. But no — God had chosen her and she alone must save France.

But how could she help France? She pleaded that she could neither read nor write, that she knew nothing about war. The heavenly voices assured her that God had chosen her for the work and insisted that she alone must do it. They promised that they would guide and help her. For more than three years, the voices gave her no peace. Time and again, in church, in the field, in the forest, the saintly visitors came to the holy girl and always they brought the same message.

### 3. JOAN ACCEPTS HER MISSION

Finally, when she was seventeen years of age, Joan yielded to the urgings of her heavenly friends. As soon as her decision was made, she lost no time in starting on her mission. St. Michael advised her to go to a near-by town and get an escort from the captain of the king's army.

Joan, accompanied by her uncle, approached the captain. The soldier laughed at the foolish idea of a simple, unschooled shepherdess saving France. He told her to return to her flocks and fields.

But Joan did not return. She waited in the town for a few days. Her brave spirit and simple piety won the love and admiration of the townspeople. Before many days had passed, she had found loyal friends among the captain's soldiers. She decided to face the old warrior again. This time he listened more attentively to her story and was inclined to help her.

All doubts, however, left his mind when a messenger rode into camp with the news that the king's army had been defeated several days before. Joan had told him this on the very day it happened, and only God could have given her the information. The captain soon appointed soldiers to escort Joan to the king.

#### 4. Joan Hastens to Meet the King

It was a happy, smiling group that bade farewell to the city. The people cheered the maid of Domrémy as, clothed in her coat of mail, she sat upon her prancing charger and rode through the cobblestoned streets. At her side were brave soldiers, proud to be the first followers of the Savior of France.

Out through the city gates they dashed and along the road to Chinon. Joan saw going before them the golden armor of St. Michael and the shining crowns of St. Margaret and St. Catherine. From that moment, there was no doubt in the mind of the soldier-maid. She knew that God was with her. Why should she fear?

For almost two weeks they rode. Poor roads and flooded rivers could not hold them back. On and on they went, over hills and through forests, now turning their course along the swampy bank of a river and now galloping over long stretches of rolling fields. Their hearts beat with joy when, at last, they beheld the gray towers of Chinon, the city where the king held his court. Joan sent a messenger in advance to the king to tell him that she had come from distant Domrémy to meet him and that she was the bearer of good news.

Soon Joan and her party rode into the city. The

townsfolk gazed in amazement as they saw the sturdy maiden in her coat of mail, riding her horse like a skilled soldier. The tongues of her friends could not hold back the secret of her visit. News so dear to the heart of the people spread like wildfire. Shouts and cheers of joy greeted Joan on every occasion.

"Hail to the Maid of Domrémy! Hail to the Savior of France!"

## 5. Joan at Court

The day arrived upon which Joan was to meet the king. With her escort, she appeared before the entrance to the great stone castle. Two heralds met her and preceded her to the audience chamber. The heavy hand-carved doors were slowly opened. One of the heralds stepped in and, after bowing to Joan, called out in a loud voice, "The Maid of Domrémy."

The sight that greeted Joan's eyes dazzled her. For a moment, she saw nothing but a gorgeous colorful mass of uniforms, dresses, pictures, and lights. Remembering that she was a soldier with a great message, she quickly recovered herself. The uniforms took the shape of living men, knights, earls, dukes, and bishops, in their silks and velvets of every color in the rainbow. The dresses began to live as the beautiful women of the court in their gayest and most charming gowns. The pictures were rich tapestries and oil paintings in heavy gold frames. The lights were tallow candles, hundreds of them, burning in sparkling crystal chandeliers. Was it any wonder that Joan was dazzled? She had never been outside her native village before; neither had she ever read of the dreamland of fairy princes.

Every eye in that vast hall was fastened on Joan. Tall and erect in her coat of silver mail, she stood before the court like a messenger from heaven. With the stride of a soldier, she walked through that brilliant gathering. The hearts of lords and ladies were thrilled through and through.

The Maid paid no attention to the crowned figure on the throne. Her keen eyes searched the crowd. She halted before a man dressed as a simple knight and in true military fashion saluted him.

"Good prince," she said, "may God grant you many years."

It was to the king she spoke. He had dressed himself as a knight and placed another man upon the throne, in order to deceive her and to test her. He protested that the man on the throne was king, but Joan could not be deceived.

For a moment there was silence. King Charles gazed at the brave Maid who fearlessly stood before him. "Pray with whom have I the pleasure of speaking?" he asked.

"They call me Joan, the Maid," she replied. Then in a clear firm voice she continued: "I come as a messenger from God to help you and your kingdom. The King of heaven bids me tell you that you will be crowned at Rheims."

A promise of help from God! That sounded good to the weak, cowardly king. He called his advisers before Joan. She answered their questions to their satisfaction and assured them that she would drive the English from Orleans if they would give her the soldiers. A shepherd maid at the head of the armies of France? Impossible! Many of the advisers warned the king not to yield to the wishes of Joan, but the king believed in her.

## 6. COMMANDER OF THE FRENCH ARMY

Joan was sent to another city to appear for an examination before other leaders of France. These were old, prudent men, but they were soon convinced that God was going to use this holy maid to help their country.

She was given charge of a small army of brave and loyal soldiers. Clad in silver armor and mounted on her white steed, she proudly took command of her forces and sallied forth carrying her showy white banner. Her very appearance inspired love and courage in those who followed her.

"Onward to Orleans," she commanded.

The historic city of Orleans had been surrounded by the English for seven months and was about to surrender.  The loss of this city would be fatal to France, and until now there had seemed to be no hope of saving it.  The British were driven from several towns along the line of march and in a few days the white banner of Joan was flying near the doomed city.  Fear was struck into the hearts of the English.  They had heard about the silver-clad Maid whom God had sent to save France. Every assault of her little army made the British quiver.

After nine days the British beat a hasty retreat and Joan with her forces entered the city.  Cannons roared and church bells rang out the joyful message of victory. The inhabitants went wild with enthusiasm as St. Joan with her banner rode to the cathedral to thank God for victory.

## 7. On to Rheims

Like a truly great general, Joan kept her enemy on the run.  "Onward and forward," was her watchword.  There was to be no rest until her work was done.

With her army she set out for Tours to meet the king. After much difficulty, she induced him to march to Rheims for his coronation.  Joan preceded him and drove the English from their strongholds along the path.  But despite all her victories, the king proved a coward and Joan had almost to force him to continue the journey.

The leader of the king's troops dispatched a messenger to the city to have all things prepared for the great event. The army was met outside the gates by a large throng of people who heartily cheered the king and Joan, the Savior of France.

Side by side through the narrow streets, they rode to the great cathedral. The line of march was decorated with banners and flags. From every church tower, the bells chimed forth in joy. Men, women, and children in holiday dress acclaimed their king and their savior with shouts and cheers.

The cathedral was a blaze of glory. Garlands and banners swung from lofty arches. Bishops in their glowing purple robes, nobles of the kingdom in their gala attire, and the Maid in silver armor gathered about the throne upon which Charles VII was crowned king of France.

"Long live Charles, our king! Long live the king!" burst in lusty shouts from the happy people as the new-crowned king stood before them in his royal robes.

But the people did not forget the Maid who stood beside the throne with her banner in her hand. They knew that it was Joan who had made that day possible, so the name of Joan was joined with that of Charles. The heart of the shepherdess of Domrémy

ST. JOAN AT THE KING'S CORONATION

was happy. She had filled the English with fear, driven them from many of the French cities, and had brought her king to Rheims for his coronation. Her grateful heart thanked God for her victory. She had now accomplished what the voices had commanded her to do.

## 8. BEFORE THE WALLS OF PARIS

But Joan was not satisfied. She wanted to drive the English from the land and to conquer the French rivals of Charles. She resolved to attack Paris, where the enemy remained in power. The king's advisers opposed her plans and the king himself gave only a half-hearted consent.

Joan and her little army made the assault. Bravely they fought with the odds against them. Again and again they attacked the city. Finally, when victory was within their grasp, King Charles ordered a retreat. Imagine how this command crushed the heart of Joan! Retreat on the verge of victory! Retreat after the battle had been fought and almost won!

But, like a good soldier, Joan obeyed. She withdrew her troops from Paris.

## 9. JOAN IS CAPTURED

The retreat from Paris was the beginning of her end. Her enemies in the king's council were working for her ruin.   In the church of St. Denis, she left her silver coat of mail and her sword as a thank offering to God Who had guided her thus far.

Her heavenly voices had warned her that her day of doom was not far distant.   Although she saw the future and was aware of the bitter opposition of those who hated her, she did not shrink from her determination to carry the good work as far as possible.   Here and there her forces attacked the English or the French enemies of Charles until she was finally captured and cast into prison.

The rest is a sad, sad story.   Neglected and forgotten by the king, scorned by his ungrateful court, she remained in chains for nine months in a gloomy prison.   Joan, the Savior of France, forgotten by her friends and tormented by her enemies!   She was condemned to be burned to death as a witch and a heretic. In vain did she declare her innocence.   In vain did she plead for a fair trial.

## 10. The Savior of France Is Condemned to Death

Joan, the saint and martyr, was bound to a pillar in the market place of Rouen and burned to death. As the flames broke from the wood beneath her feet, she cried out in anguish to the people: "Good simple people, I am innocent.   I call upon you to be my witnesses that I die innocent. I beseech you to remember me in your prayers."

The flames leaped higher and the curling smoke almost choked the "Lily of France." "Priests," she continued through the flames and smoke, "I beg you to offer a Mass for the repose of my soul. If there be any here whom I have wronged, I ask their pardon."

Then, gazing about at those who condemned her, she said, "If there are any here who have wronged me, I forgive them." She followed the example of her great Master by forgiving the very ones who planned her death. She fastened her eyes on a crucifix which a friendly priest held before her. Her body was soon hidden from view and through the flames came the faint sound of her last words: "Jesus! Jesus!"

In 1920 St. Joan was declared a saint by the church of which she was such a loyal and devoted member. The entire kingdom of France and the rest of the world rejoiced at the honor which was being done to the Maid of Domrémy. Saint, patriot, and soldier, she has won the love and admiration of the nations.

SOMETHING TO DO

Find the sentence or sentences in the story which show whether these statements are right or wrong.

1. Joan was a bright girl in school.
2. She was a delicate child.
3. Joan loved to pray.

4. She obeyed the voices immediately.
5. She was brave and fearless.
6. Joan did not recognize the king in the audience chamber.
7. King Charles was a brave man.
8. Joan drove the British from Orleans in seven months.
9. The king bravely supported her attack on Paris.
10. In the end the king proved very ungrateful.

# BLESSED THOMAS MORE

(1477–1535)

## 1. The Mass Server

"The lord high chancellor of the kingdom of England should never lower his dignity by serving Mass," said the Duke of Norfolk to Sir Thomas More, who had just served Mass in the royal chapel. "You insult and dishonor your master, the king."

"Good sir," replied Sir Thomas, "I consider it a high honor and my greatest joy to serve at the altar of my God. His majesty, the king, has no reason to be offended, for I am serving his heavenly Master."

The proud old duke only grunted in response and disappeared.

Sir Thomas never felt that he was too great or too powerful to serve Mass. Time and again, he set aside his rich robes of ermine and satin to put on the plain white surplice and black cassock of an altar boy. Indeed, so great was his love for the Holy Sacrifice that even an order from the king would never induce him to leave the church until the Mass was finished.

## 2. Sir Thomas Makes His Choice

Sir Thomas More was lord high chancellor during the reign of Henry VIII. He lived in the troubled days of the sixteenth century, the days of the great persecution in England, when those who remained faithful to the true Church of Christ were punished with suffering, imprisonment, and death. The wicked king had made himself head of the English Church. All those who opposed him were brutally punished.

The fatal day came when the lord high chancellor had to make his decision. He had to choose between his faith and glory, power and wealth — between death for his religion and a life in the highest position the kingdom had to offer. Riches, power, and glory would have attracted many another man and caused him to deny his faith, but for Sir Thomas More there was only one possible choice. Never for a moment did he hesitate. He prized his soul and his faith above any gift that the king could bestow upon him.

The king was enraged at the stand of Sir Thomas. He was cast into prison. The jailer told him that he had six weeks in which to change his mind.

"Tell those who sent you," answered the prisoner, "that I am ready to suffer death if the king so wills it, but I shall never change my mind in six weeks or in six hundred years."

This firm answer was not pleasing to the king, who really liked Sir Thomas and did not wish to see him put to death. Henry, therefore, sent Lady More to her husband to try to induce him to change his mind.

She shuddered as she entered the gloomy cell and was surprised to see her husband so happy. She told him of the king's latest promises, of all the honors that the king would give him if he would admit that the king was head of the Church. Picturing for him a pleasant honorable life as the greatest man in the kingdom, she begged him for the sake of his home and family to swear to the new Church laws and to forget his foolish notions.

Sir Thomas listened patiently to the pleadings of his wife. He loved her dearly and he loved his children with a tenderness and devotion that is seldom equaled. When the dejected wife had ended her pitiful plea, he said to her: "The life you describe would, indeed, be a happy one. But how long do you suppose I should enjoy that life?"

Lady More thought that Sir Thomas was yielding. She replied, "You will enjoy at least twenty years more of life. Your health has always been good and you will live to a ripe old age."

Fixing his eyes upon her, Thomas asked, "And what then?"

Lady More lowered her eyes because she realized

what her husband meant. No answer came from her trembling lips.

Then Sir Thomas spoke to her: "My dear wife, it is you who have foolish notions and they would still be foolish even if you were to offer me twenty thousand years. What, I ask, are twenty years or twenty thousand years compared with eternity that has no end? Shall I sell an eternity of happiness in the next world for twenty years of glory here? Oh, I pray you, think no more of it."

### 3. THE TRIAL

Weary weeks passed and Sir Thomas was finally brought to trial. As a prisoner and a criminal, he was led by armed guards into the courtroom where, as a judge, he had so often sat in royal splendor. Sir Thomas bowed respectfully to the judge who was to preside at his trial. In a loud, clear voice, the clerk read the charges against the prisoner. He was accused of refusing to believe that Henry VIII was the head of the Church in England.

The judge arranged his flowing robes and rose from his bench. He had no reason to demand silence in that crowded courtroom. The only sound that broke the painful silence was the muffled sobs of those who loved the former lord chancellor. Glancing about the room, the judge read on the faces of the people the love and sympathy that they felt for Sir Thomas.

BLESSED THOMAS ON TRIAL

In a deep bass voice, he spoke slowly and solemnly to Sir Thomas. "Sir Thomas More," he said, "you stand before the court of his royal majesty, Henry VIII, king of England. You are accused of refusing to admit that his royal majesty is the head of the Church of England. The clerk will call to the stand those who will testify against you."

A few witnesses appeared, but their testimony amounted to nothing. The judge, however, seemed satisfied. Turning to Blessed Thomas, he said, "What have you to say in defence of yourself before sentence is passed?"

Tall and stately, Sir Thomas rose from his place in the prisoners' dock. His pale thin face showed the effects of his days behind the prison walls. His body was weak and tired, but his spirit was strong and brave. The prisoner began to speak and the hearts of the throng almost stopped beating. His voice was low and soft at first, but gradually gained power until it made the hall reëcho. It was the voice of a man about to be condemned to death that spoke. He openly professed his faith in the Catholic Church and the pope. With all the enthusiasm and zeal of a martyr, he told his hearers that loyalty to that Church and its teachings is the only means of salvation. He thrilled his audience through and through. They longed to clap and cheer but dared not.

The judge grew nervous and feared an uprising of the people. Hurriedly he condemned Sir Thomas to death and ordered him taken back to jail to await his execution. Shackled like a thief or murderer, he was led to prison between two guards. A third guard followed behind, carrying the ax with its edge toward Sir Thomas, to show that he was a condemned criminal.

## 4. THE LAST DAYS

As the party drew near the entrance to the jail, Margaret, the beloved daughter of the condemned man, rushed through the crowd and threw her arms around his neck, sobbing, "Oh, my father! My father!"

Sir Thomas could hardly hold back his tears. He embraced his favorite child, but his heart was too full for words. "God bless you, my dear," was all that he could say before the guards rudely brushed the girl aside.

On reaching the jail, Sir Thomas wrote her a loving farewell note. He wrote it with a piece of coal, because his pen and ink had been taken from him. "A peck of coals," he wrote, "would not be enough to make pens to write how much you consoled me."

In his dreary cell, Blessed Thomas awaited the day upon which he was to give his life for his faith. The thought of being a martyr for Christ brought joy and peace to his heart.

His last day upon earth arrived. Holding a small cross to his heart, he was led through the streets of London to Tower Hill, where he was to die. A kind old woman met him on the way and offered him wine. He refused the drink saying, "My Master was given vinegar and gall." With tear-stained eyes and prayerful lips, men, women, and children followed that mournful procession up the hill of death.

The only happy person was Sir Thomas himself. He smiled at death and joked with those who were to put him to death. Like a child at play, he climbed the ladder to the scaffold. For a moment he knelt in prayer and then placed his head upon the block. A few strokes from the ax and all was over. Blessed Thomas More had given his life for Christ and had joined the glorious ranks of the martyrs.

### See How Much You Know

1. Compare the duke and Sir Thomas.
2. Read the sentence that shows how much Sir Thomas loved the Mass.
3. Why were people persecuted in England during the days of More?
4. What choice did Sir Thomas have?
5. Did it take him long to make up his mind?
6. How did the king try to force him to change his mind?
7. In what way did Sir Thomas differ from his wife?
8. Of what crime was Sir Thomas accused?
9. Why did the judge fear an uprising among the people?
10. What thought made the last days of Blessed Thomas happy?

# SAINT FRANCIS XAVIER

*(1506–1552)*

## 1. The Children's Friend

Ting-a-ling, ting-a-ling, ting-a-ling sounded the little handbell as St. Francis walked up and down the narrow twisting streets of the Indian city of Goa. The children ran from their homes or stopped their play to greet the new priest and to follow him to his little church. Each boy and girl who joined the procession received a loving smile or a gentle tap from Father Francis. Now and again, the boys would slyly make their way to his side, hoping that St. Francis would let them ring the bell. How happy and proud the chosen one would feel as he swung the bell with all his might! The girls managed to get on the other side of their friend and struggle for the possession of his hand.

St. Francis always led the children to his church. Here he taught them pretty little songs and rhymes. They learned these quickly and loved to sing them at home and even on the street. I wonder if you can guess what the songs were? They were songs about God and His Blessed Mother.

CARLE MICHEL BOOG

ST. FRANCIS XAVIER AND THE CHILDREN

These brown-skinned children could not read or write and books would have been useless to them. They loved the songs, however, and sang them so often at home that their mothers and fathers learned about our heavenly Father. Before long, St. Francis was able to baptize thousands of men, women, and children of the city of Goa.

Father Francis was very kind to the poor. He visited the sick in their homes and often gave them medicine that cured them. Indeed, at times he brought the sick and dying back to health through his prayers. He was beloved by all, pagans and Christians alike. Was it any wonder, then, that the hearts of the people of Goa were sad when they heard that Francis was leaving them to bring others into the church of Christ?

## 2. THE WANDERING MISSIONER

St. Francis had gone to India to spread the gospel of Jesus Christ far and wide. He resolved to make no city or town his home. From village to village, from country to country, he was to journey, converting and baptizing thousands. From Goa, he traveled to the pearl fisheries along the southern coast of India. The simple people of this region had not seen a priest for eight years and many had fallen back into their old pagan ways. St. Francis preached among them with such zeal and piety that he won them back to the faith.

Spending a week here and another there, he walked from place to place until he put new life into these neglected Christians. Idols and pagan temples were destroyed. Chapels were built. At the end of a year, he left a thriving Catholic settlement.

The missionary spirit of St. Francis now prompted him to visit other tribes. Almost everywhere he went, success followed him. It is said that in one month he baptized ten thousand people. At times he performed miracles to impress the people with the power of the God he loved and served. On one occasion he brought a dead man to life. Seeing this, the people marveled and were glad to follow him.

Daily he could be seen going from one mud hut to another, visiting the sick and encouraging the poor. God's blessing seemed to rest in every house he entered. The good Father Francis was scarcely ever alone. The people always knew where he was and kept him busy blessing their sick, giving advice to the doubtful, and consolation to the sorrowful.

It was the same story no matter where the saint went. If there was not enough rain, the people begged Francis to pray for rain. If it rained too much, they asked him to plead for dry weather, sure that God would answer his prayers.

## 3. THE RESCUE OF A CRUCIFIX

One day Francis and a companion were traveling by boat to a distant village. A terrible storm arose that tossed the boat violently to and fro. The passengers and the hardened sailors turned pale with fear and begged St. Francis to pray for the storm to end. The saint removed his crucifix and, tying it on a string, dropped it into the water. He knelt in prayer with the frightened Indians about him. The waves tossed and rolled in wild fury. The crucifix was dashed up and down until the string broke. Much to the sorrow of Francis, the crucifix sank to the bottom of the sea.

The storm kept up until late into the night. The following morning the sea was calm. The waves were rolling quietly along the bosom of the sea. The captain turned the boat towards the shore so that Francis and his companion could land. The two friends walked a short distance along the shore.

Suddenly St. Francis cried out in amazement: "Am I dreaming? Do you see what I see — my precious crucifix in the pincers of a crab?"

Sure enough on the sand before them lazily crawled a brown crab, holding St. Francis' crucifix between his pincers. The happy priest took his cross and pressed it to his lips. Kneeling upon the sand, he thanked God for this proof of His love.

## 4. The Apostle of Japan

With the passing of the years, thousands and thousands of the people of India embraced the faith of Jesus Christ through the efforts of St. Francis. When he brought a little village or tribe into the church, he always selected several of the better men to carry on the work after he had left. These he carefully instructed in the truths of religion, so that they could become teachers of the people and preserve the faith when no priest could be had.

Often while he was laboring among the people of India, stories reached the saint about Japan, the island in the northern seas where no Christian had ever set foot. Millions and millions of pagans lived and died there without ever hearing of the great God Who reigns on high. An ardent desire to preach the gospel of Jesus Christ in Japan filled the heart of St. Francis, but he found no chance to leave India.

At length, he came across Hanshiro, a Japanese merchant who had taken refuge in India. Hanshiro became interested in the religion of Francis and soon was baptized. He told Francis wonderful stories about Japan that increased the saint's longing to go there. Hanshiro explained how dissatisfied the people in Japan were with their pagan religion and how gladly they would welcome the gospel of Christ. Francis felt that he could delay no longer. A few weeks later, the apostle of India and his Japanese friend were on a boat sailing for Japan.

The holy missioner lost no time in getting permission from the emperor to preach to the people. Before many months had passed, many of the important nobles had been converted. Their good example paved the way for the conversion of the poor. Bitter opposition on the part of the pagan priests made the work of St. Francis difficult and sometimes almost impossible. With the grace of God, however, Francis did very well. When he left the island about two and a half years later, the Christians were numbered by the thousands.

### 5. THE LAST JOURNEY

In the days of St. Francis, the Japanese were great admirers and imitators of the Chinese. They looked to China for culture and education and gladly accepted whatever received the approval of China. This fact was brought to the attention of Francis time and again when he was preaching to the Japanese.

"The religion you preach," they said, "can not be very good because the Chinese know nothing about it."

Remarks like this turned the saint's thoughts to the large country to the west. He resolved to bring the gospel to China. No white man was permitted to enter that vast, rich country, but this law did not discourage the missioner. Some of his Japanese friends told him that it would be useless to try to enter the forbidden land. Death was the penalty for breaking the law. But nothing could force Francis to change his mind. He took passage on a boat for the island of Sanchan, off the coast of China. From here he had planned to enter the country secretly.

The island was reached safely, but Francis had to wait for a Chinese friend who had agreed to land him secretly on the coast of China. This delay was fatal to God's missioner. He was stricken down with a fever. With no home nor friends, Francis lay upon the bare ground, burning with fever and racked with pain. His patience and suffering brought tears to the faithful Chinaman who remained with him. No sigh nor murmur of complaint crossed his holy lips. He knew that Christ, his Savior, had suffered more for him.

A friendly Christian heard of the sad condition of Francis. His heart was filled with sympathy when he saw the suffering saint lying on the ground. With the help of a Chinese, he carried St. Francis into his little hut.

The good man did all he could for his sick guest but to no avail. The fever grew worse and, in a few days, St. Francis died. He died at the gate of the great heathen land that he wished to bring into the church of Christ. His body was shipped to Goa, the city he loved, and there it remains to-day in a beautiful silver shrine.

QUESTIONS

1. Why did St. Francis teach the children of India by songs?
2. How did the children help to convert their parents?
3. Why did Francis not remain in one place?
4. How did he make the people listen to him?
5. Tell the story of the rescue of his crucifix?
6. Mention two reasons why Francis was not as successful in Japan as in India.
7. What led him to China?

# SAINT ALOYSIUS

*(1568–1591)*

## 1. THE LITTLE SOLDIER

"Company halt!" shouted the hoarse voice of the drillmaster. With a sharp clack, the tramp-tramp-tramp of the thousand feet instantly stopped. The old warrior glanced over his soldiers for a moment and his weather-beaten face showed signs of satisfaction. "Lower arms!" he commanded. Five hundred pikes were lowered to the ground with a thud.

The drillmaster smiled kindly at the little mascot who stood before the troops with his shining helmet and his tiny coat of mail. Erect and silent like a true soldier, the child awaited the next order. Raising the boy in his arms, the old soldier embraced him, saying, "You will be a great general some day."

The little fellow was Aloysius, the son of the Count of Castiglione. The boy was only six years old, but his father wished to inspire him with a love for the soldier's life, and having decked him out like a real soldier, he had brought him to camp with the army.

One afternoon, the soldiers were dozing in their tents. The terrible heat of the Italian summer prevented their drilling. Soldier Aloysius, however, had no intention of sleeping. He wanted to play around the camp. Like all boys of his age, he had a craving for loud noises and fires.

The boy had often watched the soldiers practice with the guns and the small cannons. "Oh, if I could only make a big boom like the soldiers," he thought. The idea gave him courage. He knew where the powder was kept, and he slyly made his way to the place, hoping that the sleeping soldiers would not awaken. The boy worked fast. In a few minutes the thunderous roar of a small cannon sent its deafening noise throughout the neighboring country.

Aloysius was thrilled with joy. He ran to the startled soldiers, clapping his hands and shouting, "I did it. I made the cannon boom. I'm a real soldier now."

The soldiers were amused by his trick. Not so the father of the little culprit. Only the pleadings of the soldiers kept him from thrashing his son soundly.

Little Aloysius was a favorite around the camp. Each tent felt proud to entertain the boy-soldier. But, sad to say, he heard the soldiers cursing and swearing and, like many other boys, he imitated his elders in their wrongdoing. The rough soldiers paid no attention to the boy when they heard him use vile language like themselves.

ALOYSIUS SHOOTS OFF THE CANNON

One day when his mother was entertaining visitors, she was shocked to hear his language. She blushed with shame; her guests looked horrified.

"Where did he hear such words?" his mother demanded of the boy's tutor.

"In the camp," was the reply.

The little offender was taken aside and told how wrong it was to use such language. His face turned crimson and he cast his tear-filled eyes upon the floor. "I didn't know it was wrong," he said. "I thought that I would be like a real soldier and use all the words they use. Never, never again, will I do it."

Years and years later, the remembrance of that day always brought sorrow to his heart.

## 2. AT THE COURT OF THE GRAND DUKE

When Aloysius was nine or ten years old, his father brought him to the city of Florence, where he was to be trained in the court of the Grand Duke. Aloysius was to be his father's heir, and, as such, would live in the society of great rulers. His father was anxious that the future count should be prepared for his high position.

In the famous court of Florence, Aloysius met and played with the children of other great families. But the boy was too pious to care much about the elegant dress and manners of the court, and the life he saw there displeased him. He resolved that he would never spend his life as those about the court spent theirs.

The more St. Aloysius thought about these things, the more anxious he was to live his own life the way he wished. One day he was visiting the shrine of the Blessed Virgin in the beautiful church of the Annunciation. Casting himself on his knees, he opened his boyish heart to his heavenly Mother.

"O dearest Mother of my Lord," he prayed, "you are the purest and sweetest of all women. You are always glad to help your friends in this world. I want you to help me. To-day I promise your divine Son that never during life will I offend Him by any impure thought, word, or deed. No impure word or story will ever cross my lips. No impure action shall ever stain my soul. Oh, help me, sweet, sweet Mother!"

It was only a boy scarcely eleven years old who prayed. Yet, so fervently did he pray that all during the remaining years of his life, he faithfully kept the promise that sprang from his boyish heart. Surely his heavenly Mother protected and guided him.

### 3. In the Service of the Spanish Prince

Aloysius spent two years at Florence. Then the Count of Castiglione brought his family to Spain, for he was related to the royal family of that country. Aloysius and his brother were appointed pages to the Spanish prince. This honor delighted their father.

The boys were given a chance of being educated by the tutors of the royal family. Aloysius studied, played, and danced with the other pages and the royal princes and princesses. But the life in the palace had little that really attracted him. He was more sensible and more pious than the other pages and frequently chided them for some of their little sinful ways.

At times, the more wicked pages taunted Aloysius for being good. His blood would boil and many a time he could hardly keep from thrashing them.

A day never passed that St. Aloysius did not greet his God with his morning prayers. No day ever came to a close that Aloysius did not kneel beside his bed and recite his evening prayers. He found time each day to pay a visit to our Lord in the royal chapel. During these visits, he would speak to our divine Lord as to a kind and loving father. He unburdened his heart before the tabernacle. It was here that he felt called to serve God in the Society of Jesus.

The proud count had a violent temper. When he heard that this idea was in the mind of his son, he raved in anger and abused all who came near him.

"My son, a priest! A Jesuit!" he cried out. "Never! Never as long as I live!"

## 4. Proving a Vocation

Soon after this, the Spanish prince died. Aloysius and his brother returned to Italy with Count Ferdinand, their father. Aloysius was now about fifteen years old and the saddest period of his life was about to begin. Determined that his son and heir would never be a priest, the count sent for friends, priests, and bishops to persuade Aloysius to change his mind or to convince him that he could serve God just as well in the world. The poor boy was tormented time and again by their questions and their pleadings. Month after month, it was the same old story, but the saint always remained firm. He was determined to give up his right to his father's title and to join the Jesuits.

For two years or more, Count Ferdinand did all in his power to force his son to change his mind. At length he saw that his efforts were useless. He became convinced that God was really calling his son to the priesthood.

One evening he called Aloysius to him. "My son," he said, "all my hopes for the future were centered upon you. In my dreams I had often looked forward to the day when you would be the great ruler of our house. But now my hopes are gone. God calls you. Follow that call with your father's blessing."

Aloysius embraced his father and kissed him. For years he had prayed and hoped to hear those words.

## 5. In the Jesuit Monastery

At the age of eighteen, therefore, Aloysius found himself in the Jesuit monastery at Rome, where young men are trained for the priesthood. A little room, with a flagstone floor, one plain chair, and a hard bed, became the home of the son of the Count Ferdinand. He had given up a title, a palace, servants, luxuries of every kind to serve God in a whitewashed cell. But he was happy in his new home, happier than he had ever been before.

The monastery, with its poverty and its bareness, was the home of Aloysius for the next five years. Here he prayed and studied. Here he obeyed all the rules of the house. His piety and charity made him loved by his companions. There was nothing unusual about his life here. He did the simple, ordinary things, but he did them perfectly. He studied well; he prayed well; he played well; he obeyed the rule well.

When St. Aloysius was about twenty-three years of age, a terrible plague broke out in Rome. Hundreds and hundreds of the people of Rome fell victims to this dreadful disease. Death followed death until the number became alarming. The Jesuits, those loyal, brave soldiers of Christ, opened a hospital. The priests and brothers nursed the sick and dying, washed their running sores, made their beds, and served their meals. Yes, at times they even had to dig graves to bury the dead.

The thought of helping the poor, suffering people filled the heart of Aloysius with joy. He begged his superiors to permit him to assist in this wonderful work. At first, his request was denied because he himself was not in good health. But the saint was so persistent that his superiors yielded.

The son of Count Ferdinand became the nurse of Christ's poor. Oh, how he loved to soothe their pains! How gently he washed their ugly sores! How careful he was when lifting them not to increase their pain! He fed the weak and was never too tired to give drink to the thirsty.

### 6. ALOYSIUS BECOMES A VICTIM

Before long, the disease attacked Aloysius. Everyone knew that his weak body could not overcome the sickness.

He became weaker and weaker until finally he was confined to bed. He was patient and resigned to God's will. He often spoke of his death with joy, because then he would be joined with Christ Whom he loved so dearly on earth. His superiors saw that his strength was fast giving out. Each day he grew paler.

A devoted friend sat beside his cot and read to him some of his favorite prayers.

"I shall die to-night," Aloysius whispered to the friend one evening. "Read the prayers for the dying."

The priests gathered in his little room and recited those beautiful prayers that are said for souls that are about to appear before their God: "Depart, O Christian soul, out of this sinful world and let peace come to thee this day, and let thy abode be with God in heaven. Through Jesus Christ our Lord. Amen."

The dying saint whispered the answers to the litany. When the prayers were finished, he thanked those who had gathered about his bed. The superior thought that he looked well and would linger till morning. He asked two priests to remain with Aloysius for the night, while the others retired.

The dying youth was wiser than his superior. He knew that he would not see the light of another day. He asked his companions to pray with him. A lighted candle was placed in his hands and his crucifix was laid on his breast.

"Into Thy hands, O Lord, I commend my spirit," prayed the dying saint. "Sweet Jesus receive me. Holy Mary pray for me. O God, I believe in Thee; I hope in Thee; I love Thee; I am sorry for all my sins. My Jesus, mercy! My Jesus, mercy!" His voice grew weaker and weaker. At length it could be heard no more.   The candle trembled in his hand.   St. Aloysius closed his eyes and was no more.

### CAN YOU ANSWER THESE?

1. How was Aloysius like most boys?
2. Mention the two places to which Count Ferdinand brought Aloysius for training.
3. What did St. Aloysius think about life at the court?
4. Was Aloysius faithful to his prayers?
5. How did his father try to prevent him from joining the Jesuits?
6. What did Aloysius give up in order to study for the priesthood?
7. Do you think his death was a happy one?   Why?
8. In what ways can you imitate Aloysius?

# SAINT VINCENT DE PAUL

## (1576–1660)

### 1. VINCENT'S EARLY YEARS

The De Paul family lived in southern France. There were six children in the family, and William, the father, often found it hard to feed and clothe so many. His only means of support was a small farm. The children were trained when quite young to help about the farm. In the early morning they drove the cattle to the pastures and brought them home after sunset. The boys went up and down the rows of beets, peas, and carrots and pulled out the weeds, while the girls helped around the house and prepared the vegetables for the market.

One of the children seemed to be better and brighter than the others. This boy's name was Vincent. He understood things more quickly and did them better than the other children. His father resolved to send Vincent away to school, because there was no means of getting an education in the little village. Mr. De Paul knew that he would have to save and skimp to do this, but he felt that the sacrifice would be rewarded later. He often dreamed of this clever lad as a famous doctor or lawyer who would take care of his parents in their old age.

Vincent was sent away to boarding school. The board and tuition were less than thirty dollars a year, but Mr. De Paul found it hard to save even this small amount. Good reports came to him about the success of Vincent. The father was proud of his boy. On Sundays after Mass, he always lingered in front of the little stone church, waiting for some of his farmer friends to ask about his son.

Vincent was an industrious lad. He appreciated the sacrifices that his family was making for him. He prayed that God would speed the day when he could help them. The days of his boyhood were soon over and, being a pious youth, he decided to study for the priesthood. This meant more years of schooling and more money, but St. Vincent had a strong faith in the goodness of God. "I shall do the very best I can," he said, "and let God take care of the rest."

Before long, Vincent was asked to act as tutor to some small boys who had entered the boarding school. Because of his kindness and learning, his pupils increased until he could pay his own expenses. It was a happy day, indeed, when the burden of his education was lifted from the shoulders of his poor parents.

Year by year, through trials and poverty, he was approaching the greatest day of his life, the day of his ordination. It came and went, leaving Father Vincent a happy, holy priest. Born and raised in poverty, he had gained by prayer and perseverance the greatest honor that can come to man on this earth.

## 2. CAPTURED BY PIRATES

Soon after his ordination, the good news reached him that a friend had died and left him some money. "How good God is," he exclaimed. "Now I can pay my debts and have a little left over for the poor."

With the first money he received, he wished to help those who were worse off than himself. It was the beginning of that great love for God's unfortunates that made him known throughout the world as the apostle of the poor.

To collect the money, Vincent had to go to Marseilles. In order to save money that he might have more to give to the poor, Vincent took passage on a boat for the return journey, rather than return by train, which was more expensive.

There was no pleasure for the boy raised on the farm in watching the boat plunge up and down in the dashing waves. When the ship had been plowing through the foamy water for some hours, the young traveler became seasick. His face grew pale and he sank into a deck chair and prayed that the journey would soon come to an end.

The end came sooner than expected. Father Vincent noticed the crew on the boat hurrying excitedly around the deck and looking through spy glasses toward the west. He felt that something was wrong. Jumping from his canvas chair, he ran to the captain and asked the cause of all the excitement. The terror-stricken captain made no effort to answer but continued to shout his orders to the crew.

"Turn the boat toward the shore and sail with all possible speed," he cried.

Vincent soon heard the excited sailors talking about the pirates who were chasing them. The alarm quickly spread among the passengers, and frantic women ran around the deck crying and praying. Vincent really saw no reason for fear. Pirate stories had thrilled him during his school days and he thought that it would be interesting to watch them search the boat for booty and return without any. His mind had already settled on a hiding place for his money. But all this showed that Vincent did not know very much about Turkish pirates.

The French sailors saw that the Turks were gaining ground. The captain watched the men as they pulled at the sails with all their might. The old boat, however, could not be made to hurry. It plowed slowly along. The captain looked behind and saw that the race was hopeless. The swarthy faces of the savage Turks could be easily seen. Nearer and nearer they

CAPTURED BY THE PIRATES

came.   Soon their fierce shouts to surrender reached
the ears of the frightened Frenchmen.

The disheartened captain thought that there was
only one hope and that was to fight.   He ordered the
crew to seize their bows and arrows and shower darts
upon the approaching enemy.   Yelling and shouting,
the Turks drew their boat alongside the French.

"Surrender or death," called out the chief of the
brigands, brandishing a shining scimitar on high.

The answer was a stream of arrows from the French
bows.   A few of the Turks fell to the deck pierced with
arrows.   This attack angered the pirates.   They were
skilled in the use of the arrow and their aim was far
more deadly than the aim of the French.   They returned the assault, and several Frenchmen dropped
wounded or dead.

By means of ropes and ladders, the brigands boarded
the ship.   The chief ordered the captain put to death
immediately for daring to fight them.   The passengers
and members of the crew were bound with cords and
chains and brutally beaten and placed upon the pirates'
boat.   Father Vincent, bound and lashed, had changed
his ideas about pirates.

### 3. Sold as a Slave

After spending several days plundering boats along
the coast, the brigands returned to Tunis, their home

on the northern coast of Africa. Here the prisoners were marched through the streets of the city, accompanied by a Turk who shouted to the passers-by that the captives would be sold as slaves at the market place in the afternoon.

Imagine how Father Vincent felt when he heard that he was to be sold as a slave! Just a few weeks before he had been ordained a priest. For years he had looked forward to the day when he would work among his people as another Christ. Now his hopes were blasted. His dreams were banished. He was to be a slave — a slave among bloodthirsty infidels who hated Christ and His Church.

That afternoon, Vincent was sold to a gruff old fisherman, who lived in a little hut near the sea. This old man spent his days and nights upon the water. Fishing in the deep sea was good and he had made a great deal of money selling his fish in the market place of Tunis. Now he thought that he would make his task lighter by having a slave do his work. But he had picked the wrong man in Vincent.

Every time they sailed out to sea, Vincent got very seasick and could do nothing but lie in a heap on the bottom of the boat. The angry fisherman lashed him and beat him, but it did no good. Vincent had not been made for the sea. His master was disappointed in his bargain and soon sold him.

Vincent's new owner was a chemist and life with him proved happy for Vincent. The chemist was kind to him and soon learned to love him. Together they worked and talked in the shop, as the master tried experiments with his acids and metals. The conversation often turned to religion, and at times heated arguments arose between the Christian slave and the Mohammedan master. St. Vincent, with all the fervor of his noble spirit, defended his faith in the God Who died on Calvary to save mankind. The chemist listened with interest and he was forced to admire the courage and zeal of his slave.

One day, he said to Vincent: "You would make a wonderful Mohammedan. Join our religion and I shall give you your liberty and make you my heir."

The wealth of the chemist appealed to Vincent and his freedom was very precious. But wealth and freedom amounted to nothing when weighed in the balance with his faith.

"Your wealth is great, indeed," answered Vincent, "and I prize my liberty above any other earthly blessing, but remember that my faith is dearer to me than all the gold in Tunis. I love it far more than life. Gladly would I die rather than deny it."

The master smiled upon his slave and loved him all the more for his loyalty to his religion.

It was a sorry day for Vincent when this good man

died, and his possessions passed into the hands of his brutal nephew. Vincent's new Turkish master saw that the slave was worth a great deal, so he sold him to a Frenchman. This man was a traitor who had given up his religion and his country to live as a Turk.

### 4. THE FRENCH TRAITOR'S SLAVE

Vincent was sent to work in the cornfields. From early morning till long after sunset, he worked with his hoe and sickle among the rows of tasseled corn. The hours were long and the African heat was burning. How different everything was from his father's farm in France! But Vincent went patiently about his work. He made himself forget his trials and sufferings by singing hymns and chanting his prayers to the music of the wind as it rustled and waved the drying stalks of corn. His mind often wandered back to the dear little village church in France where the people gathered to sing the sweet songs that he loved so well. The hymns he had learned at college echoed in his ears.

One day, his master's wife heard him singing the "Hail, Holy Queen." She was so impressed by the fervor of the song that she asked him to sing it again for her. Often, after this, she had him repeat the beautiful hymn to her. Her interest was aroused in the religion of the captive and, from time to time, she questioned him about his Church. So well did St. Vincent explain the teachings of the Church to her that she upbraided her husband for giving up such a wonderful faith.

Whenever Vincent had a chance, he spoke of religion to his master and tried to bring him back to the God Whom he had deserted.

The old traitor often blushed with shame and hung his head, saying, "I have gone too far for the mercy and pardon of God."

The holy priest reminded him that God was a God of mercy Who came into the world to save sinners. Little by little, the grace of God worked in the old man's soul, until one day he said to Vincent: "I would give all that I have to be back again in my dear France, united with the God I used to love. Since the day I denied my God, my life has been filled with sorrow and disappointment."

## 5. THE ESCAPE FROM AFRICA

But it was no easy task for the old man to break the bonds that bound him to his Turkish masters. Spies watched his movements, ready to kill him if he turned traitor to the Mohammedan faith that he had adopted. With Vincent, he planned and schemed to return to France, but the eyes of the Turks seemed to be everywhere.

One dark night, however, the two Frenchmen cautiously picked their way over the twisting mountain roads to a narrow footpath.  The path led to a small seaport where boats sometimes called on their way to France.  At the sound of a footstep or the echo of a human voice near them, they hid themselves in the tall, leafy bushes.  Fortune favored them.  They were able to make the journey in safety and they soon boarded a ship that brought them to their native land.

When the boat reached France, Vincent and his companion knelt upon the sandy shore and thanked God for their escape.  The sinner who had given up his faith was reconciled to God and spent the rest of his life in helping the poor.

## 6. LABORING FOR THE POOR

We next hear of St. Vincent as the tutor of the children of the Count de Gondy, a wealthy and prominent Frenchman.  Vincent's piety and learning soon began to show itself in the children under his charge.  The Count and his wife often thanked God for their good luck in having such a tutor for their children.

Life at the palace, however, with its luxuries and its good times, was not to Vincent's liking.  He loved the poor, the ignorant, and the downtrodden, and he was anxious to work among them.  He begged the bishop to send him to some poor neglected village.

Before long, he was given charge of a small town where most of the people had forgotten about God and His church. Father Vincent gathered four or five other zealous priests about him. These holy apostles set themselves to the task of bringing souls back to God. From door to door they went, talking to the poor, sympathizing with them, helping them, and urging them to come back to church.

The results were not pleasing at first, but the priests kept preaching and praying until the little town took on a new life. Now when the church bell rang, the people hurried to hear Mass and to listen to Father Vincent, the friend of the poor.

But while all this good work was going on, the Count de Gondy and his wife were planning to force St. Vincent to return to Paris. They loved him dearly and knew of the wonderful good that he would be able to do in the large city of Paris. The Count gave his brother, the Archbishop of Paris, no rest until St. Vincent had been ordered to labor in the city of Paris.

The Archbishop gave him a house where he and the priests who joined his little community might live. These holy men gave all their time to preaching and taking care of the poor and sick. Into the poorer sections of the city they went bringing food to the hungry and medicine to the sick. They soon won the love and admiration of all Paris.

## 7. The Apostle of the Poor

St. Vincent saw the need of hospitals. He and his followers went from door to door and from city to city, begging for money to build hospitals for the sick. One by one he founded hospitals in the poorer districts of Paris. A community of Sisters was established to take care of them. This community still carries on the work which St. Vincent started. We call them the Sisters of Charity.

But he did even more than this. He formed a society which had a branch in each parish. The members of this society looked after the poor and the sick in their parish. To-day the St. Vincent de Paul Society, as it is now called, is found not only in France but in parishes all over the world.

His community of priests increased and established houses all over France. Their fame for preaching made them welcome wherever they went. To-day we find them spread all over the world. They are called the Congregation of the Mission, or the Vincentian Fathers.

As the years passed, St. Vincent became the most popular priest in France, the father of the poor, and the friend of kings and queens. No one, either before or after him, has been such a valiant defender of the poor and the downtrodden.

St. Vincent was never satisfied with his work. He always felt that he had not done enough for the sick and poor. His whole life was spent for them. He planned for them. He pleaded for them. He begged for them.

In all his labors, he never forgot that he was helping the poor for the love of God. In each poor afflicted soul, he saw a brother in Christ. When he gave them food or nursed them, it was always for Christ's sweet sake.

Indeed the thought of God hardly ever left his mind. Every time the clock struck, he made the sign of the cross upon his breast and recited an act of love. No matter how busy or tired he was, he never let a day pass without spending at least three hours in fervent prayer. It was this constant union with God that made his love for God's creatures so productive of good. Even to-day he is known everywhere as the apostle of the poor.

QUESTIONS

1. Into what three parts can you divide the life of St. Vincent?
2. What lesson do we learn from his life as a young man?
3. What is the first example given of his love for the poor?
4. When did Vincent change his ideas about pirates?
5. Why did the old fisherman sell Vincent?
6. Why did the chemist admire Vincent?
7. Why did the old traitor blush with shame?
8. Among whom did Vincent like to work?
9. In what ways did Vincent help the sick and the poor?
10. What is Vincent called?

# SAINT ISAAC JOGUES

## (1607–1646)

### 1. THE ARRIVAL IN NEW FRANCE

For eight weeks the clumsy old boat with its large
weather-beaten sails had plowed through the ocean.
At times, the mighty foaming waves had rolled moun-
tain high and dashed the boat around as if it were a toy.
The passengers and crew were glad indeed that the
stormy voyage was over as they sailed up the broad
St. Lawrence River and approached the bluffs at
Quebec.

The courteous captain stepped aside as the gang-
plank was lowered at the docks. "Father Jogues,"
he said, addressing a young Jesuit priest, "you are
to be the first passenger to go ashore."

The missionary shook hands with the crew, thanking
them for their kindness during the voyage and stepped
ashore. A small group of fellow priests had gathered
to welcome him to New France, as Canada was then
called, and he was soon laughing and joking with them.

That night, before retiring, he sat beside the crude
fireplace, and by the light from the glowing embers
he wrote a letter to his mother. He knew that she

would be worrying about him and praying for him until the news of his safe arrival reached her.

"I do not know the joys of heaven," he wrote, "but I do know that no earthly joy could be greater than the joy that was mine when I first stepped on the shores of the New World."

He was happy, indeed. For years he had prayed that God might hasten the day when he could spend his life converting the Indians. For years he had dreamed of leading the savage redskins to the feet of Christ.

## 2. THE FIRST MISSION

After a few days' rest in Quebec, Father Jogues started up the St. Lawrence with a group of Indian guides and companions in a long line of canoes. He was on his way to the Huron tribes on Georgian Bay. It was a long, tiresome journey of about twenty days. Now they paddled along rivers or sailed through lakes, now they carried their canoes and supplies over swampy portages. During the entire journey, they were on the alert all the time, lest some hostile tribe might capture them and steal their supplies.

Father Jogues reached the mission in good health, but in a few days he was taken ill with a high fever. This gave him his first taste of real mission life. His fellow priests peeled some bark from near-by birch trees and spread it in a corner of the floor of their home.

Rushes were scattered over this and covered with bear-skin. This was the sick bed of Father Jogues.

There was no doctor nor medicine at hand. Day after day, anxious companions watched and prayed at the bedside, as their friend hung between life and death. Someone suggested the old popular remedy of drawing off the blood of the sick person. Father Jogues himself opened a small blood vessel and let out some blood. Whether this helped him or not we do not know, but at any rate, he gradually grew better and the fever finally left him.

In a few weeks, he was visiting the Indian villages with another Jesuit priest. Even though he could not speak the language of the Hurons, he won their friend-ship by his smile and his kindness to their sick and dying. On these journeys, he was often called upon to baptize infants who were about to die or to instruct adults in the faith with the help of the little he had learned of the Indian tongue. The thought that he was spreading God's kingdom on earth brought joy to his heart and well repaid him for all the hardships he suffered.

Chief among these hardships was the fact that he and his companions were always in the shadow of death. The Indians were a superstitious race and readily blamed the Blackrobes, as they called the priests, when anything went wrong. When things were going well,

ST. ISAAC PREACHES TO THE INDIANS

they were glad to have the priests near them. But just as soon as any sickness or plague broke out in a village, they blamed the missionaries. At these times, they often drove them from the villages and threatened them with death.

Father Jogues had been working scarcely a year among the Hurons when a plague spread through the tribe that caused the death of many. The blame was immediately placed on the holy Jesuit, and he had to go in hiding until the fury of the savages died away.

Now and then, the priests were accused of being devils or of having evil spirits. The anger of the redskins would be roused against them and their only safety was to keep out of sight for a while. But in spite of all this, the zeal and courage of God's messengers continually increased. The Indians admired this bravery and many became fast friends of the Blackrobes. Soon among the wigwams appeared little log mission chapels, where Indian braves with their squaws and papooses worshiped the true God.

### 3. RUNNING THE IROQUOIS BLOCKADE

It was now three years since Father Jogues and his companions had heard from Quebec, the source of clothes, food, medicine, and other supplies. Their clothes were worn to rags. They needed food and medicine for themselves and the Christian Indians.

But the trip to Quebec was a dangerous one. They had to run the blockade of the Iroquois, the most warlike of the Indian tribes.

With death from cold and starvation facing them, they resolved to attempt the journey. Father Jogues took charge of the expedition. In their bark canoes, they paddled along the lake in safety until they entered the region where the Iroquois were hunting. They became more cautious now, hiding by day in bushes along the shores and by night silently and swiftly traveling through the dangerous places. Not a word was spoken as the paddles noiselessly cut the cold blue water and forced the light barks onward. It was almost a week before the expedition felt safe in traveling during the day. No mishap befell them and, midst the cheers of their friends, they arrived safely at the fortified city of Quebec.

### 4. IN THE HANDS OF THE ENEMY

A few days of rest at the fort and the travelers were on their homeward journey with their canoes loaded with clothes and supplies of all kinds. Their success in avoiding the enemy on the way down gave them courage now. As much as possible, they skirted along the shore in the shadow of bushes and tall grasses. For five days, there was no sight of the enemy. It seemed that the Iroquois had withdrawn from the Great Lakes.

Just after dawn on the sixth day, Father Jogues suddenly gave the signal of danger. Iroquois spies were sighted some distance ahead, hiding in the underbrush. The missionary and his companions turned their canoes around and gained the land as soon as possible. The boats were pulled up on the marshy shore, out of sight of the spies. The travelers crouched on the ground behind some wild shrubbery, hoping that they had not been seen.

For a little less than an hour, they waited, anxiously listening for any sound of the approaching enemy. Suddenly from every direction they heard the noise of the crunching of leaves and the cracking of twigs.

"We are surrounded," cried Father Jogues. "Be brave. We may outnumber them."

The arrows from a hundred bows showed that the enemy came in large numbers and that there was no hope of escaping through the woods.

"To the canoes! To the canoes!" shouted the priest. But there was no need of the order. His companions were already pushing the boats into the water.

Just then a number of Iroquois boats appeared from behind the curve and showered the fleeing Christians with arrows. Surrounded on water and land, there was no hope of escape. They surrendered to the enemy.

## 5. A LIVING MARTYR

Dancing a war dance about the disheartened captives, the Iroquois hooted and shouted in glee. After brutally beating their victims, they bound them with leather cords and cast them into canoes. Then began their triumphal journey through the rivers and lakes of upper New York to the stronghold of the tribe at Auriesville, near the present city of Albany.

It was here that the terrible torture of Father Jogues and his companions took place. With clubs and iron rods, the priest was beaten without mercy. Each Indian brave tried to strike harder blows than his neighbor on the body of the captive. Some of the young men of the tribe yelled with delight as they plucked the beard from the priest's face and left him covered with blood. Others tore off his finger nails. Little jeering boys danced around the poor missionary as they jabbed him with hot irons. In patience and silence, this saintly hero bore all these sufferings.

But when a wicked, wrinkle-faced old squaw began to chop off the thumb of his left hand, he cried out for mercy. He pleaded and begged her to beat him or burn him but to spare his thumb. The evil woman laughed at his tears and sneered at his pleadings. With a rough knife, she hacked the finger from his hand and then threw it at him in contempt.

Little did the squaw dream the reason for the tears of the priest. They were not tears of human weakness. The missionary looked forward to the days when he would gain his freedom and when he would again offer up the Holy Sacrifice on the altar of God. But with his consecrated finger cut off, he would be forever deprived of that joy. Was it any wonder, then, that tears, real manly tears, rolled down his tanned cheeks when the Indian woman refused to listen to his plea?

The brutal savages were not content with inflicting so much misery on their prisoner. The leaders of the tribe met and decided to put him to death. Dutch fur traders from Albany heard of the sad plight of the priest and saved his life, but he refused to flee with them. He had hopes of converting the Iroquois.

### 6. A WILLING PRISONER FOR GOD'S SAKE

Father Jogues was now adopted as a slave by one of the Indian families. He built their fires, helped to cook their food, and carried heavy burdens as they moved from place to place. He had given up home and friends for the love of those who made him a slave.

For more than a year, this holy Jesuit remained a slave among the savages. Even though he was carefully watched, he could have escaped at different times. But there was no thought of escaping in his mind. The

Dutch traders often wanted to help him but he refused all aid.

"I cannot desert my companions," he said. "Although a slave and a captive, I have many chances of doing good. I baptize the dying and save many a soul from hell. At times, I secretly instruct some of the adults in the faith."

Even when the French government tried to obtain his release, he wrote, "I prefer to remain as a captive unless it be the will of God that I escape." Some time later, however, his life was in danger and the Dutch governor insisted on helping him to escape. The poor priest spent the whole night in prayer seeking the will of God. After finishing his prayer, he felt that it was God's wish that he should save himself.

## 7. FREE AGAIN

Father Jogues fled to Albany and later succeeded in reaching New Amsterdam, now the city of New York. It was hopeless for him to attempt to return to his friends in the North, so he sailed for France.

His arrival in his native land was the cause of much excitement. Everyone, even the queen, wanted to see the holy priest who had been tortured so cruelly. He did his best to steal away and hide from the gaze of the curious who called him saint and martyr.

The missionary's health was soon restored and he

longed to celebrate Mass again. The law of the Church forbade him to do this because of the loss of his consecrated finger and the cutting of the others. His superior appealed to the pope for special permission. The permission was readily granted by the Holy Father, who said that it would be improper to prevent a martyr of Christ from drinking the sacred blood of his Master at the Holy Sacrifice.

The bitter suffering and cruelty that Father Jogues had endured did not change his missionary zeal. In a few months, he was back again in New France, working among the French and the Huron Indians around Montreal.

The Iroquois were still on the warpath against the French. At the most unexpected times, they would attack French settlements, killing the inhabitants and escaping with the loot. It was never safe to travel between villages without armed guards.

The French governor was weary of these attacks. He tried to make a treaty with the Iroquois. Several Indian chiefs met the French to make terms of peace. The speaker for the French was the former captive of the Iroquois, Father Jogues. Both sides promised peace and good will.

The French commander, however, was suspicious of the good intentions of the Indians. He wanted to be sure of peace. Some months later, therefore, he sent representatives with gifts to the Indian chiefs, telling them how pleased the French were with the peace. Again Father Jogues was the spokesman for the French. As he gazed upon those savages who knew nothing about God, his old desire to convert them started to burn again. He resolved to return and work among them.

## 8. THE FATAL BOX

On departing for Canada, he left with the Iroquois a box containing vestments and other religious articles, telling them that he would soon return. Sad to say, this box was the cause of his death. A pestilence broke out among the Indians that killed many. The corn crop was a failure. The poor Indians blamed all this on the box that the Blackrobe had left behind. They said that it contained an evil spirit that had brought all this misery on them. It was decided to put the priest to death on his return.

It was some months before the holy priest arrived. Weary and hungry, he entered one of the Indian villages. The sullen faces of the squaws told him that something had gone wrong. A sulky grunt was the only response to his greeting.

Fleet-footed Indian boys ran to the near-by river where their fathers were fishing to tell them that the Blackrobe had returned. The braves raced to see who would be the first to capture the priest. What a surprise for him when he saw six redskins dashing for him with anger in their eyes! They bound him with leather cords and beat him until blood covered his body.

"What have I done to merit this?" he said. "I thought that I came as a friend to friends. Did not your noble chiefs sign the treaty of peace with the white man?"

Making wild gestures with their muscular arms, they exclaimed: "White man no good. No corn now for red man. Why? Because of white man. Our Indians die. Why? Because of white man. White man no friend of red man. He leave black box with evil spirit and bring sadness to our people. White man must die."

"You judge me wrongly," protested the Jesuit. "I come as your friend. I gave up my home and friends to live with you and help you. I came to be kind to your sick and to teach you about the Great Spirit, the God of the white man. The box that you complain about has nothing in it but the vestments that the Blackrobe uses when he worships his God."

The Indians gazed at him in silence. He knew that this meant that they had not changed their mind. Death faced him at any moment. In his hut, he prayed that night: "O God, I came as Thy servant among these neglected Indians. If it is Thy will that my days be ended so soon, let Thy holy will be done. I gladly give my life for them. Have mercy on them, O God, and bring them within the bosom of Thy church."

The next evening as Father Jogues was entering his wigwam, a powerful Indian brave smashed his skull with a tomahawk. The other redskins shouted in glee as the murderer cut the head off and hoisted it upon an iron pole in the village. The bruised body of the holy man was then thrown in the river.

There are few examples in all history of braver souls than Saint Isaac Jogues. After tasting the horrible torments of the savage Iroquois, he returned, fully aware of their treachery, to bring to them the faith of Jesus Christ. Torture and death held no fears for him! He came to preach the gospel of peace and, like a true hero, died bravely in the attempt.

In June, 1930, Pope Pius XI placed the name of Isaac Jogues among the saints of the church.

### TRUE AND FALSE

Number a paper from 1 to 10. After each number place X if the statement to which it corresponds is true or 0 if the statement is false.

1. A steamboat carried Father Jogues to Quebec.
2. The sea was very rough.
3. Father Jogues was thoughtful of his mother.

4. The village doctor cured him.

5. He did not begin work till he learned the Indian language well.

6. The Indians hated the priests because they were cowards.

7. The Hurons were the most warlike of the Indian tribes.

8. Jogues and his friends were captured on their return from Quebec.

9. The squaw cut off the little finger of Jogues.

10. Jogues never said Mass again.

# SAINT GERARD MAJELLA

## (1726–1755)

### 1. THE PLAYMATE OF THE CHRIST CHILD

One summer morning, some people went to pray in the village church in the Italian town of Muro. In the silence of the deserted church, fervent prayers ascended to the throne of God. The slamming of the church door startled the worshipers. They turned around and saw a smiling lad about five years old tripping up the center aisle. They wondered where the little fellow was going.

Imagine their surprise when they saw the child throw a friendly kiss at the statue of the Blessed Virgin and then kneel before it in prayer!

But this was nothing compared with what followed. The Infant Jesus left the arms of His Mother and came down to play with His visitor. For some time the two boys frolicked about and laughed as only boys can. The Infant Jesus then returned to His Mother's arms and gave His friend Gerard a little loaf of snow-white bread. With the wave of a chubby hand and another kiss, Gerard hurried home with his gift. He told his family that the Mother of his little playmate in the church had given him the bread.

The next morning, his sister followed him and entered the church without Gerard knowing it. She hid behind a pillar so that she could watch her brother without being seen. Gerard again greeted his new friends with a kiss and was soon playing with the Christ Child. The girl hurried home to tell her mother of the wonderful sight she had seen.

## 2. Gerard's First Communion

Little Gerard often knelt in church and watched his family receive Holy Communion. He could not understand why he was not allowed to receive with them. He said: "God loves little boys and I love God. Why won't God come to visit in my heart?"

His love for Jesus was so great that he thought he would never be able to wait for his twelfth birthday, the age when children in those days were permitted to receive Holy Communion.

One day while attending Mass, he followed the older people to the communion rail, thinking that God would surely tell the priest to give him Holy Communion. The priest looked at the small child and passed him by. Gerard's heart was broken. Leaving the church, he hurried home to cry his little heart out where no one would see him.

But his heavenly Father was watching him. God was so pleased with his love and devotion that He sent St. Michael, the archangel, to bring Holy Communion to the boy saint.

As the boy Gerard grew older and learned more and more about God and His Church, his love for the Blessed Sacrament increased. No day was ever too short or too busy for a visit to the lonely Prisoner in the tabernacle.

### 3. Gerard the Lay Brother

When Gerard became a young man, he joined the Redemptorist community as a lay brother. Daily he went about the monastery, cooking, sewing, cleaning, and tending the garden. Many of those about him thought that the new brother was a sort of simpleton. Before long they were forced to change their opinion and admit that Gerard was not a fool but a saint blessed by God.

Strange things began to happen in the monastery. Miracles took place almost daily through the power of Gerard. Even in the common ordinary things of life, it was not unusual for Gerard to use his wonderful power.

A certain village blacksmith could give proof of this. One day St. Gerard was on a tour begging for the monastery. From farm to farm and from town to town

THE DONKEY KICKS OFF HIS NEW SHOES

he went, riding an old donkey.   On arriving at a certain village, he noticed that his donkey had lost her
shoes.

He soon found a blacksmith who replaced the shoes,
but the price he demanded for his labor was so high
and unjust that St. Gerard refused to pay it.   He commanded the donkey to kick off the shoes.   The beast
raised one foot and then another, flinging the shoes
near the anvil.   The blacksmith let the hammer fall
from his hands and gazed in amazement as St. Gerard
mounted his donkey and departed with a smile.

### 4. Gerard Takes a Journey on Faith

St. Gerard had wonderful faith in the goodness and
generosity of God.   He knew full well the meaning
of our Lord's words, "Ask and you shall receive; seek
and you shall find."   No matter what the need or difficulty, Gerard was always sure that God would send
him help.

A very interesting story is told that shows this marvelous faith in God.   About ten students at the monastery were anxious to make a pilgrimage to a famous
shrine that was several days' journey distant.   The
rector regretted that because of the expense he could
not grant the permission to the students.   At the time,
there was very little money at the monastery.

The youths pleaded earnestly and suggested that

Brother Gerard would take care of the trip. The rector instantly recalled the many miracles of the holy lay brother, so he told the students that they could go under the care of Gerard.

Some extra clothes and food were packed on two donkeys. Brother Gerard counted his money and found that he had about two dollars. Two dollars to pay for the food and lodging of eleven people for a week! Any other person would refuse the task, but Gerard never hesitated for a moment. He knew that God would provide.

Things were all ready, but the balky donkeys, true to form, refused to move. They were pulled by the halter and beaten with rods, but they did not budge. The owner complained that they were too tired. St. Gerard would not let two stubborn donkeys delay his journey. Seizing a whip, he gave each a crack, saying, "I command you to go in the name of the Holy Trinity." The donkeys immediately started and trotted along without any further trouble.

It was hot summer weather and climbing the dusty Italian roads tired the youthful travelers. St. Gerard suggested using a carriage.

The students laughed at his foolishness, saying, "How can we ride in a carriage when we have not enough money for food?"

Gerard replied, "The Lord will provide."

A carriage was hired to take the party to the next town. How the boys welcomed the rest! They wondered, however, how Brother Gerard would get enough money to pay for the ride. They grew a little nervous as the carriage halted in the town square and the time to pay the fare was at hand. They fastened their eyes upon Gerard to see what he would do.

Like a man with unlimited means, he asked, "The amount, sir?"

The driver thought that his passengers did not have much money, so he said, "Three dollars will be enough."

The youths bit their lips. That was more money than they had started with! But Brother Gerard calmly opened his old leather purse and handed the man three crisp new bills. The boys breathed a sigh of relief. They were indeed thankful and knew that God was helping their friend.

Gerard turned to his companions and said: "We still have a little money left. Let's buy some flowers for the altar with it." This suggestion did not sound good to the students. They told him that it would be better to buy them some food, because they had eaten scarcely anything all day. Gerard reassured them with his "God will provide."

Flowers were bought and Gerard went with his friends to make a visit to our Lord in the parish church. The holy lay brother placed his gift on the altar. With childlike simplicity, he knelt down and prayed, "Dear Lord, you see how good and thoughtful we have been of You. It is now your turn to show how good You can be to us."

As he spoke these words, the sacristy door opened and a tall, thin priest appeared. He greeted the visitors and invited them into his home. "I shall do the best I can," he said, "to get you something to eat and to make you comfortable. If my dear mother were not ill, you would fare better."

Brother Gerard thanked the good priest for his kind offer but hesitated to accept his invitation because there were so many in the party. However, the priest insisted and, much to the delight of the boys, the invitation was accepted. St. Gerard called the priest aside and said to him, "I am sorry that your mother is not well, but if you make the sign of the cross on her forehead, she will be cured."

Hurrying home, the pastor did as requested and his mother was instantly cured. The visitors were happy and their hungry mouths were filled with good things to eat. They thanked their host heartily and departed with an extra gift of money lying securely in the treasurer's purse.

On and on, the joyful boys proceeded, surprised each day by another proof of the wonderful power of Gerard. Having reached the shrine, they thanked God with all their heart for the many gifts He had given to them.

On the homeward journey, the travelers spent a day climbing mountains. They were tired and thirsty, and they were delighted when they saw a well some distance from the road. In true boyish fashion, they raced to see who would be the first at the well. A gruff farmer sat near the well and told them that they must pay for the water.

This angered Gerard. "We have no money," he said, "to pay for a free gift of God." He argued with the man but in vain. "Very well then," said the saint, "the God Who filled that well will now empty it. You have sold your last drink."

Disappointed and more thirsty, the party continued along the dusty road. They had not gone far when they beheld the farmer racing after them.

"In the name of heaven, come back! Come back, I pray you! My well has gone dry."

Gerard and his friends returned. The sign of the cross brought the cool, clear water back to the well. The farmer fell at St. Gerard's feet and begged for pardon. He had learned his lesson and, to show his gratitude, he insisted upon filling each cup for the parched youths.

At the end of a week, the saint led his companions back to the monastery. The loud laughter and talking of the boys brought the priests and brothers to the large reception room. All the boys were talking at once, each trying to give an account of the wonderful trip. When the priests turned around to congratulate the friend of God, he could not be found. He had quietly slipped away to the chapel to thank his Friend for all He had done for him.

To the end of his short life Gerard continued doing in the same quiet way those marvelous things that showed God's special love for him. Never seeking praise nor thanks, he went about doing good until the very end.

CAN YOU DO THIS?

The following words describe people and things in the story. Copy the list, placing after each word the name of what it describes.

| | | |
|---|---|---|
| 1. Italian | 5. marvelous | 9. hungry |
| 2. smiling | 6. balky | 10. boyish |
| 3. snow-white | 7. sudden | 11. gruff |
| 4. marble | 8. thin | 12. dusty |

# THE CURÉ OF ARS

*(1786–1859)*

## 1. THE BOY PREACHER

It was a peaceful, happy scene that God looked down upon from His throne in heaven. Sheep were quietly resting under the shade of spreading oak trees and lazily munching the newly-sprouted grass. With their gentle bleating they answered the birds that twittered in the trees above them. Several little shepherd boys were on their knees before a small statue of the Blessed Virgin. With their shepherd's staff in one hand, they prayed to heaven's Queen. How fervent and sweet were those childish prayers that angels carried to Mary!

From the group rose a serious-faced boy, scarcely nine years old. In his hand he held a statue of the Mother of God. Turning to his companions he spoke to them earnestly, telling them of the love they should have for the Mother of Jesus. A holy light seemed to shine about his face as he urged his little friends to love and honor the Blessed Virgin.

As the boy-preacher left them to lead his sheep toward the brook, his companions remarked, "Surely Jean-

THE LITTLE PREACHER

Marie will be a great priest some day." Little did the shepherd boys know that their friend was later to become one of the greatest priests in God's church.

## 2. Childhood Days

God gave Jean-Marie a pious mother who carefully watched over her boy. Day after day, he would sit at her side as she told him about God and His saints. In his childish heart she placed great hatred of sin, and later, in times of danger and temptation, his mother's words always echoed in his ears. "My dear little Jean-Marie, if I were to see you offend God, it would grieve me more than anything else in the world." Was it any wonder that a boy who had such a mother became one of the great saints of the church?

As a child, Jean-Marie delighted to hear Mass in the little stone church of the French village where he lived. His eyes never left the altar from the beginning to the end of Mass. By his own actions, he tried to give a lesson to some of his careless companions who talked or looked about during the Holy Sacrifice. The people of the village noticed his piety and often urged their children to imitate him.

In school Jean-Marie was always slow. He studied well but he was never so bright as the other boys and sometimes his companions taunted him by calling him "dunce." Even when he grew older, he had the greatest difficulty in remembering what he had been taught, and in the seminary the teachers decided he was too ignorant to be ordained. When this message was given to him, it almost broke his heart. All his life he had wished to be a priest, and each day he had prayed to God to help him be a good priest. But now, just before his ordination, he was sent away as a hopeless dunce.

One of his friends went to see the bishop to ask his help. He told the bishop that although Jean-Marie had never been bright in school, he had the heart of a saint. The good bishop paused for a moment. He thought of all the good work a zealous priest could do, even though he were not bright. He recalled the poor, simple fishermen that our Lord chose as His first priests. The bishop then sent a message to the priest in charge of the seminary, telling him to prepare Jean-Marie Vianney for ordination.

### 3. Pastor of the Village of Ars

When St. Jean-Marie had been a priest for about two years, the bishop sent him as pastor to the little village of Ars in southern France, saying: "There is very little love of God in Ars, Father Vianney. Go and put some there."

The bishop's words were all too true. Ars was indeed a wicked place where the people had forgotten about God. The parish church was deserted but the dance halls and drinking houses were always filled. To this sinful people, Sunday was the same as any other day of the week.

As the young priest walked through the narrow streets of the village, men, women, and children paused in their work or play to gaze at the new pastor in pity or contempt but scarcely ever in reverence or in love. This grieved Father Vianney greatly. He loved those sinful souls and gladly would have laid down his life to save them. Hours and hours he knelt alone in the silent church, begging our dear Lord to help him win these poor souls back to Him.

But there were a few faithful souls in Ars, and with them he started his work. He spoke fervently to them about the love for Jesus that should fill their hearts. He pictured the lonely Savior on His throne on the altar without a friend or visitor. He told them that, from day to day, Jesus waits in His prison home to welcome those for whom He came into this world. So lovingly and earnestly did the holy priest speak about our Lord that tears trickled down the cheeks of those who heard him. He pleaded with them to show their love by joining a society in honor of our Lord in the Blessed Sacrament. They promised to have someone kneel before Our Lord in His prison home each hour of the day. This was the seed that blossomed forth into a wonderful society for adoring Jesus in the Blessed Sacrament.

## 4. THE VILLAGE BEGINS TO CHANGE

The first few friends of the new Curé, as the holy priest was called, were so impressed by his zeal and piety that they urged their friends to hear him preach. In his quiet simple way, he won the hearts of all who knew him. The village folk soon greeted him in a more friendly manner when they met him. Little by little, the number of people at church increased.

The good priest never rested in his search for souls. Like a good shepherd, he sought out the careless and the hardened sinners and, by kindness, brought them back to the church. It was in the confessional that he did most of his good work. From near and far, people came to the quaint little town of Ars to seek the advice and sympathy of the holy Curé. His Christlike spirit brought soul after soul back to God. Sometimes he heard confessions for more than fifteen hours a day. His heart was always overflowing with love and kindness toward the sinner. In his simple way, he pleaded with them to be loyal to their Savior and never to grieve His Sacred Heart by sin. Hardened sinners are known to have left his confessional in tears.

One day a fellow priest asked him about the penances he gave in confession. The Curé smiled and answered, "I give easy penances and try to do the rest myself." In truth, his life seems to have been one long penance. He wore his cassock until it almost fell off him in rags. For years, his only food was boiled potatoes, black bread, and water. His bed was hard and his hours of sleep few. When visitors came to eat with him, he always managed to serve better food and pretended that he was enjoying it himself.

It is said that for twenty-five years he conducted an orphanage by merely trusting in God. When money was equired to pay for things, he prayed and asked God to help him. Help always came. Once the Sister Superior told him that the food had given out and she had nothing left but a few pounds of flour. The Curé told her to place the yeast in the flour and fix the dough as usual. The Sister did as he commanded. Later, when she was placing the dough in baking pans, she found that she had enough dough to supply the orphans with bread for several days.

### 5. The Closing Years

During the later years of his life, the Curé's work became so difficult that the bishop sent several other priests to help him. People came from all over France to see the holy Curé of Ars, to listen to him preach, and to go to confession to him. Each year thousands and thousands of people filled the village church. Often men and women remained all night in the church while the poor, tired Curé heard confessions. He was often known to rise at midnight during his last years and go to the church to hear the confessions of those who were waiting for him. At times he was so weak that he had to be carried from the confession box to his bed.

The holy man had now grown old and gray in the service of the Master. The food he ate was not sufficient for the hard, tiresome work he was doing. His strength was failing rapidly, but he kept at his work till the very end.

When the news spread through the country that the holy Curé was dying, the prayers of those who loved him pleaded with God to spare him. But his time had come. Before long the bronze bell in the church tower rang out slowly and mournfully to tell the people that their father, friend, and guide had gone to his eternal rest.

Unknown and unwelcomed, he had entered the wicked town of Ars as a young priest. Now, an old, worn-out man, he left it a village of holy people who loved and revered the kind, lovable priest who, by his holy life, made Ars known throughout the world.

QUESTIONS

1. Can you give two examples to show how Jean-Marie tried to influence his companions. How can you influence your companions?

2. In times of temptation what words did Jean recall?

252 HEROES OF GOD'S CHURCH

3. Can you prove from the story that Jean was not discouraged because he did poorly in school?

4. Which do you think the bishop valued more, piety or knowledge?

5. What command did the bishop give to the Curé on sending him to Ars?

6. Before starting his work, what did the Curé do?

7. What was the first society he established?

8. How did he do most of his work?

9. What kind of village was Ars when he died?

10. What lesson does his life teach?

# BLESSED THÉOPHANE VÉNARD

## (1829–1861)

### 1. FAREWELL TO HOME

Théophane Vénard's last farewell to his family was a sad one indeed. He loved his dear old father, his sister, and his brothers with a tenderness that is seldom found. All the joys of life seem to have been centered in them. The interesting letters that he had written while away at school showed the wonderful affection that filled his heart for those at home. And now at the age of eighteen he was saying good-by to them forever.

But for years Théophane had felt the call of his Master to labor in His Chinese vineyard. In his dreams he saw those neglected pagan souls that had never heard the sweet words of the saving gospel of Jesus Christ. The stories of the brave, holy priests who labored, suffered, and died in China for Christ thrilled his pure heart with a burning desire to imitate them.

He cast himself at his father's feet and asked for his blessing. The dear old man placed his trembling hand upon the bowed head of his beloved son. His poor heart seemed too full for words. He struggled to hold back the tears.

Remembering that his boy was answering God's call, he conquered his natural feelings and said: "A father's love and a father's blessing be with you always. May the dear Lord, Whom you go to serve, watch and guide you throughout the dangerous days that are to come."

The youth arose and kissed his father again and again. His two brothers and his devoted sister embraced him amid their sobs and tears. Their best friend was leaving them forever.

Poor Théophane could stand the agony of parting no longer. He took the clothes that loving hands had tied into a neat bundle and hurried to the buggy that was waiting to take him to the station. He waved his last farewell to the weeping family. On earth they were to meet no more.

## 2. OFF FOR CHINA

Théophane took the train for Paris where, for several years, he prepared for his work in China. The great day of his ordination to the holy priesthood came. How happy he was to hold for the first time in his hands the sacred body and blood of his God! How glad to repeat on God's altar the unbloody sacrifice of Calvary! How thrilled to know that he had the power to save men's souls from hell!

The months passed quickly and at last Théophane

was on the high seas sailing for China. For many weary weeks the vessel plowed through the rough waves, but Théophane paid little attention to the trials of the journey. His mind was on the great pagan land of the East.

Father Théophane first stepped on Asiatic soil at Singapore. In a few weeks he found himself studying the Chinese language at Hong Kong. Those who have tried to learn this language tell us that it is very difficult, but after a year of study, the bishop felt that Théophane knew enough of the language to begin his missionary work.

The young priest was appointed to the Tong-King mission, a mission in the country south of China proper. He was delighted. Secretly he had prayed and hoped for this mission, because here the persecution was most bitter and the chances of being a martyr were greatest. It meant death for a priest to enter that hostile land. Christians were punished, fined heavily, and imprisoned. But in spite of all this bitter persecution, the priests had done wonderful work and converted thousands and thousands to the faith of Christ.

### 3. IN THE TONG-KING MISSION

After receiving his appointment to the Tong-King mission, Théophane wrote a letter to his family showing the delight that filled his heart. "Think of the martyrs," he wrote, "those real glories of Tong-King, the flowers of God's garden. They are the protectors of the missions. Their blood is pleading to God for us, and the thought of their victory gives us fresh courage to fight on. Only think what an honor, what a happiness it would be for your poor Théophane to be a martyr for Christ!"

To a friend he wrote, "Every time the thought of martyrdom comes to me, I thrill with joy and hope."

For more than six years, Théophane labored among the people of Tong-King. He found the country very different from his beloved France. During most of the year, it is a swamp land, and, for at least four months, the country is completely covered with water. At this time of the year, all traveling must be done in boats.

One morning on awakening, Théophane found his one-room house flooded and fish, crabs, and frogs swimming beneath his bed. He did not mind these, but when he saw a few rats taking refuge in his bed, he thought that it was time to move higher. He called in some of his Christian neighbors and shortly his bamboo home was hoisted four or five feet above the water.

The task was an easy one because all the homes in Tong-King were very light. They were made of latticed bamboo poles plastered with a thin layer of mud.

The roof was thatched with straw or covered with dry leaves, held in place by cords and mud.   You can easily see that in those homes there were none of the modern comforts, no soft beds, nor easy chairs.

Surely with the floods, the damp, sultry climate, and the lack of home comforts, the missioners enjoyed few of the pleasures of life.   But these hardships were nothing compared to the bitter persecution they suffered at the hands of the rulers of the country.   They were never sure of their lives.   A price was placed upon their heads.   To be captured meant death.   Mandarins and village chiefs tracked them as the hunter pursues the wild beasts of the forest.   They came to preach the gospel of peace and they were treated as wicked criminals and enemies of the people.

## 4. Persecuted for Christ

How often did these messengers of God steal into their boats and under cover of night slip away from their pursuers!   How often did they conceal themselves in hiding places while the mandarins with soldiers stalked through the town seeking them!   For days and days, they would remain hidden, afraid to whisper a word, lest spies might hear them.

Many a time, they took refuge in the mountains and lived in gloomy, filthy caves without food or drink, until some faithful Christian felt safe to carry them something to eat. For weeks at a time, they lived in the midst of the wild animals that make their homes in the mountain forests, fearing death at any moment either from their pursuers or from the ferocious beasts. Here they would patiently wait for the news that their enemies had left that part of the country.

Yet in spite of all these trials, they brought thousands and thousands into the church of Christ. Their untiring zeal for the conversion of the pagans was well rewarded. Their converts were loyal and devout, and hundreds of them gave up their lives rather than deny the faith of Christ or betray those who had taught them that faith.

### 5. Blessed Théophane Is Captured

Like the other missioners, Théophane worked and struggled with a love that never tired. Threatened several times with death from consumption, after each attack he would return to his work with renewed vigor and zeal. Several times he almost fell into the hands of those who sought his life, but God guided him to safety. These narrow escapes never cooled his ardor. He had come to convert souls and he was resolved to do all in his power to accomplish that work.

The mandarins and village chiefs became more watchful. They were angry to think that the Frenchman could escape so often. It hurt their pride. Spies were

offered money for any information that might bring
about the capture of Father Théophane, but faithful
Christians generally warned their friend before the
arrival of the officers.

One morning, however, he awoke to find his bamboo
home surrounded by guards.   There was no chance for
escape.   Father Théophane hid behind a wall in the
house while a friend answered the chief who had knocked
at the door.

The officer was not satisfied with the answer he
received.   He knew, from the information his spies
had given him, that his victim was still in the house.
He entered and kicked over the boarded partition.
Letting out a yell of glee, he pounced upon the crouch-
ing priest and dragged him from the house.

Father Théophane was bound in iron chains like a
dangerous criminal and put in a bamboo cage.   Then
he was brought to the capital of Tong-King.

He was a prize prisoner, yet by his kind manner
he so won the love of those who met him, that he was,
to a certain extent, treated with kindness.

The next day the captive was brought before the
chief mandarin for trial.   This judge really liked his
handsome, youthful prisoner and wished to save his
life.   He urged Théophane to trample on the cross
or give some sign of giving up his faith.

The missioner smiled at this foolish request and said :

"I have taught others to die for that faith, and shall I, their leader, desert the banner under which I have fought these past years? Your prisoner will die first."

"Are you not afraid of death?" asked the mandarin.

"I welcome it," replied Théophane, "and look forward with joy to the day when I shall meet my God." The pagan mandarin could not understand the wonderful faith from which these words came.

## 6. IN THE BAMBOO CAGE

The judge admired the bravery of the young Frenchman. To make things more comfortable, he ordered a larger cage for Théophane and had it placed near the front of his home.

Armed guards paced to and fro before the cage to prevent the Christian prisoner from escaping. Many of the important people of the town came to see the captive. His gay spirits surprised them.

A few faithful Christians managed to get positions near the condemned priest. One brought him food secretly; another delivered letters to him and carried his letters to friends; still another, a priest, unknown to the guards, heard his confession, while a woman brought him Holy Communion hidden in a piece of bread.

For almost three months, Blessed Théophane lived in his bamboo prison, praying God to give the poor

THÉOPHANE IN HIS BAMBOO PRISON

pagans about him the grace to see the truth. From time to time, the guards were kind enough to let the prisoner out of the cage so that he could take a little walk in the garden. How glad he was to stretch his body!

One morning shortly after breakfast, he was walking outside his cage. A good Christian woman slyly approached him and whispered, "Father, you are to be put to death to-day." The news did not startle him because he had heard false reports so often before. He was resigned to God's will and glad to be found worthy to die for his Master.

With an escort of two hundred soldiers, he was led to the place of execution. The soldiers tied him to a stake. A few blows from the ax cut his head from his body. The blood that was shed for Christ poured upon the ground. Blessed Théophane, valiant and holy martyr of Jesus Christ, died in the year 1861 at the hands of those he came to save.

### QUESTIONS

1. Read aloud a few sentences to prove that the missioners' life was a hard one.

2. How many pictures do you see in this story? Describe them.

3. Can you suggest better titles for the little chapters of the story?

4. Can you find ten words that describe the character of Blessed Théophane?

5. Why was Théophane so eager to be a martyr?

6. Can you make an outline of the story?

# FATHER DAMIEN, THE MARTYR OF MOLOKAI

## (1840–1888)

## 1. BANISHED FOR LIFE

It was a hot summer day in the year 1873. The rays of the sun beat down upon the city of Honolulu and danced upon the waves that rose and fell in the harbor. Three large sailing boats, tied to the wooden docks, tossed gently to and fro with the motion of the water.

The wharves were alive with people. Some half clad in rags lay upon the docks and near-by shore. Others sat around in small groups or walked impatiently up and down. These were the poor lepers of the Hawaiian Islands who were being banished from their homes to the lonely island of Molokai. The government had decided that this was the only way to stop the spread of this dreadful disease.

Never before had the harbor been the scene of such sorrow. Friends and relatives gathered fondly near their loved ones. No visitors would be allowed on the leper island, so many a weeping mother tenderly embraced a daughter that she was to see for the last time; husbands kissed their wives farewell forever, and brothers and sisters were parted to meet no more.

The captain jerked the cord of the boat bell and gave the signal to load the ships. Sailors lowered the gangplanks and hurried ashore to carry the hopeless victims on board. Some struggled; many wept aloud and screamed. The heartbroken relatives fought for a last kiss but were pushed aside by the sailors. A terrible chorus of moans and cries rose from the natives as the boats bearing their dear ones sailed from the harbor.

There was only one calm person on the docks that day. A kindly-faced priest in a worn cassock quietly picked his way through the weeping lepers. With the sign of the cross, he blessed them one and all. He whispered a word of cheer and comfort to some; to others he gave a look of tender sympathy. Their pitiful moans and cries made his gentle heart bleed. The poor suffering people knew that Father Damien loved them and they loved him in return.

## 2. A Volunteer

Some weeks after this scene, Father Damien was talking with the bishop who had charge of the islands. The good bishop remarked that he was very sad because he had no priest to send to the lepers on the island of Molokai.

"Bishop," said Father Damien, "you could give me no greater joy than to send me to Molokai."

Fearing that, perhaps, the good priest was speaking without thought, the bishop answered: "Surely you do not mean what you say. Do you understand what it means to be sent to Molokai? It means that you may never be able to return and that, perhaps, you, too, may become a leper."

"Your grace," replied the priest, "I know very well what I am saying. My request is not the result of any foolish whim. For many months my heart has bled in sympathy for those poor neglected souls. My love goes out to them. Send me to be their helper and I shall be grateful as long as my life lasts."

The bishop could not resist this earnest appeal. That very day, he and Father Damien took passage on a boat sailing for Molokai. There were no sad farewells for the good priest at the docks. There were no fond embraces and kisses from relatives and friends. He had long before cut all ties that bound him to the world and its pleasures. Now he was banishing himself to live forever on an island that most men passed by with a shudder of horror.

The lepers were glad to see the bishop and their friend. The bishop visited their settlements and gave them words of comfort. Just before returning to Honolulu, he spoke to the lepers.

"My dear children," he said, "for some time you have had no priest to take care of you. But thank God, it will be so no longer. Behold I am leaving with you Father Damien, your friend, who will be a father to you. His love for you is so great that he is willing to become one of you, to live for you, and to die with you."

The boat which would bring the bishop back to Honolulu slowly pulled out from shore. The apostle of the lepers was left alone, without a companion, without a home, and without money. He had exiled himself for life for the sake of the afflicted lepers who gathered about him. For the love of God, he closed the door forever on home and friends, on the joys and comforts of life.

### 3. Life on the Leper Island

The lot of the poor lepers was, indeed, a sad one, for they were without any hope of being cured. They lived in small settlements on the island, but what villages these were! Small round huts of mud and grass were the lepers' only homes. In filth and poverty, they lived in these huts more like animals than men. Their clothes were ragged and dirty; their food poor and scant. No doctor or nurse came to visit them.

Was it any wonder, then, that the heart of Father Damien bled with sympathy for these poor abandoned

FATHER DAMIEN AMONG THE LEPERS

souls? Was it any wonder that he was sorrowful when he saw the dreadful conditions in which these outcasts were living? The task before him was a big one. It required a man strong of will and stout of spirit. It required a man of courage and perseverance. The hero of Molokai was such a man and he immediately began his work.

His first few weeks were spent in visiting the huts and taking care of those in the last stages of the disease. He washed their sores and bandaged the hands and feet that were rotting on the body. Never did the good priest fail to bring comfort and joy to the hearts of his lepers. His visit was like a soft blessing falling from heaven.

The government officers who had charge of the island lived in Honolulu and most of them had never visited the leper colony. Therefore they were not acquainted with conditions on the island. Father Damien knew that the best way of obtaining their help was to inform them completely about the conditions among the poor lepers.

After Father Damien had become acquainted with the lepers and had seen what needed to be done on the island, he returned to Honolulu to seek aid from the government. Now, people in Honolulu and elsewhere feared to come near anyone who had been among the lepers lest they themselves might contract leprosy.

So as soon as the President of the Health Department saw Father Damien and learned that the priest had just come from Molokai, he gasped in horror and shrank back from his visitor.

"How dare you come here from the leper colony?" he stormed. "If you return to the island, you will be forbidden by law to leave it again."

We can pardon the excited man because his fear of this terrible disease was so great.

"Mr. President," answered the lepers' friend, "I shall indeed return to Molokai and whenever I am able to help those poor sufferers on yonder island I shall come back to Honolulu."

He kept his word. His courageous heart would dare anything when he wished to improve the conditions under which the lepers lived. During the first few years he returned to Honolulu time and again to plead his cause before the government and in most cases his requests were granted.

## 4. Improvements

The priest's efforts to improve living conditions were first turned toward the water supply of the island. It was the old story of "water, water everywhere and not a drop to drink." The salt waves of the ocean bathed the shores of the island, but the people had no fresh drinking water. When burning fevers parched their lips, they had to drink stale rain water. Father Damien wrote several letters to the government asking that fresh-water wells be drilled on the island. The answers were too slow in coming, so he went in person to the agents of the government in Honolulu. So earnestly did he plead that his request was granted and before long the exiles were enjoying cool, fresh water.

The filthy shacks that the people used as homes filled the priest with disgust. On his daily visits through the colony, he often entered those dirty little huts and found eight or ten lepers crowded together on the mud floor. He described the terrible home conditions to the government and several boatloads of wood for building houses were sent to the island.

Father Damien now became the foreman of a group of leper carpenters who had never built anything but a mud hut before. He directed them in building wooden houses with real wooden floors. Those in the last stages of disease were moved into the new houses first. A rather large building was used as a hospital. One by one the old huts were torn down. In less than ten years, about three hundred homes were built by the lepers.

Great changes had now taken place in the colony. The poor doomed people were much happier than they had been for years. The stronger ones took care of the weak and dying. They bathed their sores and gave them food. Often they knelt beside the decaying body of a neighbor and prayed God to take him from this world of misery.

Everything on the island was now improved. The lepers were cleaner than before and their homes were neater. Of course things were not as clean and sanitary then as they are to-day. But most of the lepers took a pride in seeing that the wishes of their friend were carried out.

Father Damien saw room for further improvement. The lepers needed more and better clothing. The government sent a small supply each year, but the garments were soon in rags. At times the relatives of the exiles helped them, but there was always need for more. At Father Damien's suggestion, a clothing store was opened on the island and the government gave each leper six dollars a year for clothes. This seems a very small amount of money to buy clothes for a year, and of course it was not enough, but the people got along much better than they had before. We must remember, too, that the climate was warm and that no shoes were used by the lepers.

Father Damien now turned his attention to improving the food of the lepers. He sent a letter to Honolulu and in response received a few cows, horses, and carts, besides the regular supply of food. A message also came from Honolulu telling the priest to teach the people to make their own living from the soil.

This message angered Father Damien. He knew that those who sent it did not understand much about the soil or conditions at Molokai and he decided to tell them in person. The best of farmers cannot grow crops from rocks and sand, and crops cannot be harvested by sick and dying lepers.

Father Damien went to the agents of the government in Honolulu and explained to them so carefully and earnestly the need for better food that his request was granted.

As the years passed on, hospitals were built and doctors and nurses came to take care of the sick and dying. But no doctor or nurse brought more joy to the patients than the daily visit of Father Damien. Often he nursed them in their last illness, praying aloud with them until the angel of death freed their souls from their decayed bodies. Then, with his own hands, he made their coffins and buried them silently in the little graveyard beside the village church.

## 5. A STRANGE CONVERSION

Father Damien was always anxious that those in danger of death should make their peace with God. At times, this was indeed a hard task. In a letter to his brother, he tells an interesting story about a woman whom he tried to convert. To all his pleadings, she turned a deaf ear and, at times, laughed at him for his trouble. This, however, did not discourage him. Again and again he visited her and begged her to be sorry for her past sins and to beg God's forgiveness.

One night he was roused from his slumbers by a leper nurse who called him to the bedside of the dying woman. He hastened to the hospital. The poor, suffering woman was in the last stages of disease. She moaned, and muttered, and tossed about excitedly. The power of speech had left her. With motions of her hand, she showed the priest that she wanted to write something.

The nurse brought a pencil and a pad of writing paper. This is what the woman wrote: "I am not an evil spirit. I am the guardian angel of this woman. For several months, I have urged her to be converted, but you have seen how stubborn she has been. I have used this violent means to bring her to her senses. To-morrow she will be herself again and will be converted."

Imagine the surprise of Father Damien when he read this strange message! He folded it with a smile and placed it in his pocket, thinking that, perhaps, the woman was insane.

The next day, as he passed through the hospital, he paused at her bedside. For the first time, she

greeted him kindly and said: "Father, you have been
anxious about me during the last few months. I
spurned your kind invitations to make my peace with
God, but my insults never discouraged you. I am
deeply sorry for it all, and I beg of you to let me die
a good Catholic."

The face of the priest brightened because he had
won another soul for Christ. He handed the leper
the message that she had written the night before.
"Do you recognize this?" he asked.

She read the paper. Then she looked at him in
surprise and answered: "I know nothing about this
strange note. I never saw it before in my life."

Father Damien then told her the story of the message. A peculiar look came into the eyes of the doomed
woman.

"Oh, I see it all now," she exclaimed. "For six
months and more, a voice has been whispering in my
heart, telling me to be a Catholic. I paid no attention to it and laughed at the idea. I was resolved to
die as I had lived. The voice gave me no rest nor peace
until something strange happened yesterday. I do
not know what it was, but on awakening this morning, I wanted to be a Catholic. Instruct me, Father,
in your holy faith. May God forgive me for all the
sins of my past life. Baptize me that I may meet my
God in peace."

## 6. The Leper Priest

Twelve years had come and gone since Father Damien had begun his labors on the saddest island of the earth. Morning, noon, and night, his life had been spent with the outcasts of human society. But during those twelve years, no fear of this dreadful disease had entered his heroic heart.

Everyone thought it was strange that he had not contracted leprosy. He himself was surprised at his good fortune. He was pleased, too, because it gave him more time to help his people.

One day, however, he felt quite ill and asked for some hot water to bathe his feet. He plunged them into the water without knowing that it was so hot. On drying them, he noticed that they were covered with blisters from the scalding water although he had felt no pain.

"God's will be done," he exclaimed. "The fatal disease has laid its hands upon me."

Leprosy often begins by making the limbs numb or insensible to pain, heat, and cold. Father Damien knew the disease so well that he had no doubt about his condition. When word went around the island that the pastor was afflicted, the lepers wept. The best friend they had on earth was doomed.

The disease only made the priest dearer to his people.

For four years more, he labored among them until the awful affliction so weakened him that he had to remain in bed.

Oh, how sad it was to stand near that bedside and see the lepers in all stages of disease come to see their Father. They kissed the covers of the bed. They kissed his withered hand and through their tears asked his blessing.

As the end drew near, they knelt about the bed and chanted the litany of the dying with the priest who had come to help the dying apostle. The end came slowly. The little bell above the chapel tolled the mournful message to the people. Father Damien was dead! A brave hero and a holy priest of God's church had gone forth to receive the reward that God promises to those who love Him. He had lived and died a martyr of brotherly love.

#### How Well Did You Understand the Story?

1. What part of the story do you like best? Why?
2. Describe the saddest picture.
3. Tell how Father Damien tried to help the lepers.
4. Give five words that describe the character of Father Damien.
5. Suggest new titles for the chapters.

# SAINT THÉRÈSE, THE LITTLE FLOWER

## (1873-1897)

### 1. THE PILGRIMAGE TO ROME

It was a bright, clear November morning in the year 1887. Pope Leo XIII sat upon his throne of gold and ivory at the end of a great reception room. Tall and thin in his robes of snowy white, he was receiving the pious pilgrims from France who had come all the way to Rome to receive his blessing. One by one, they knelt in silence before the holy man as he raised his hand to bless them. To stand in the presence of the great ruler of God's Church caused their hearts to fill with pride and joy.

Among the pilgrims was Thérèse Martin, a beautiful girl of fourteen, with long golden curls falling around her shoulders. Large blue-gray eyes lit up her mild, sweet face and a touch of the rose was on her cheeks. She seemed a little nervous as she pulled at the folds of her dress. Indeed, she had good reason to be nervous. She had come to one of the great moments in her life — a moment that was to decide her future.

Ever since she was a tiny child, she had desired to give herself to the service and love of God. Day after day, from her pure, simple heart went forth fervent prayers to her Lord, telling Him how much she loved Him and how eager she was to spend her life in serving Him. It was her delight to hide herself among the pretty flowers in the family garden and build little altars where she offered her sweet prayers to Jesus and His blessed Mother. Two of her sisters had already entered the convent, much to the delight of their good father. Now his youngest daughter and his favorite was eager to follow their example.

St. Thérèse or "the Little Flower," as she is often called, wished to be a Carmelite nun. The rule of the holy Sisters who lived at the Carmel was very strict. Cut off from the world, these pious women chose to live a life of poverty and prayer in order to please God and to save souls. Their bed was a few boards with straw thrown over them. Rough sandals took the place of shoes and stockings. No meat was ever served at their table and, from day to day, they ate the simplest kind of vegetables and bread. In the middle of the night, they rose from their hard beds and gathered in the chapel to sing the praises of the Lord. Their home was behind the walls of a convent where no one might enter and from which they were never allowed to depart.

It was such a life as this that holy Thérèse chose to live. She pleaded with the Mother Superior to permit her to enter the Carmel, but, because of her youth, the permission was refused. Later, accompanied by her kind father, she went to the bishop and begged him to help her. He promised to think the matter over. The little saint became weary waiting.

As a last hope, she decided to plead with Pope Leo when she went to Rome with the pilgrims. So it was no wonder that she was twisting and pulling nervously at her dress as she stood before the pope. She knew that years of happiness depended on the answer of the Holy Father.

Again and again, she counted those in line before her. Oh, would her turn ever come! Minutes seemed like hours to her. Her little heart began to beat so fast that she feared she would faint. Just three between her and her hope! Then two! Her body trembled when she saw that her turn was next. She prayed for courage and help as she fell on her knees before the throne.

Tears filled her eyes as she looked pleadingly into the kind face of Pope Leo and said: "Holy Father, I have a great favor to ask of you." There was a hush and a moment of silence. All eyes turned towards the beautiful girl who had dared to speak to the pope. With his true fatherly heart, the Holy Father bent his head forward to hear the request. Two little white hands were clasped upon his knees and a tearful voice

St. Thérèse Pleads with Pope Leo

whispered: "Holy Father, permit me to enter the Carmel at the age of fifteen."

One of the priests who knew Thérèse was standing near. Shocked at her boldness, he explained her wish to the pope. The pope gazed for a moment at the beautiful tear-stained face and the pleading voice again broke out: "Holy Father, if you only say 'yes' everybody else will be willing."

But the prudent man would not make such a hasty decision. He blessed the Little Flower and said to her: "Well, child, you will enter if it is God's will."

## 2. ENTERING CARMEL

It was a sad girl who left Rome and returned to her home in France. She had done all in her power but had failed. However, she did not give up hope. She increased her prayers and felt sure that God would answer them. In a few short months the good news came. The bishop had sent a letter giving her permission to enter the convent at fifteen.

The great day finally arrived. With her father and her sister, St. Thérèse attended Mass in the chapel of the Carmel convent. Together for the last time, they received Holy Communion. The kind old man knelt beside his favorite daughter and knew that she would be his for but a few short moments more.

He tried in vain to hold back the tears. He was

glad and proud to give his Thérèse to God but the parting filled his heart with sorrow. The Mass was ended all too soon. Thérèse and her father walked arm in arm to the door of the convent. A kiss, a fond embrace, and a father's blessing — and then father and daughter parted. Seldom was she to see him again and, at those times, an iron grating would stand between those hearts that loved each other so dearly.

For nine months the vocation of St. Thérèse was tested. She put her whole childish heart into the keeping of the rule in all its rigor. She asked for no exception and refused those offered to her. She spent her days in doing the little things well. Thus far in her life she had done nothing wonderful or unusual, nothing that others could not do. But she loved God above all things and served Him by doing well all the little things that she was supposed to do.

### 3. THÉRÈSE BECOMES A NOVICE

During nine months she proved her fitness to keep the strict rule. Then a day was set aside when she was to be clothed in the habit of the Sisters of Our Lady of Mount Carmel. On this day the Sisters were to accept her as a member of their community. For such occasions, the Sister who is to be received into the convent is dressed as a bride to show that she becomes the bride of Christ.

Like a queen, Thérèse, in bridal dress, walked up the middle aisle of the chapel on her beloved father's arm. Her long golden curls covered her shoulders. Her graceful form was clothed in a beautiful white velvet gown with a long flowing train trimmed in rich lace. A fine lace veil fell in soft folds about her and reached the floor some distance behind. With measured step, father and daughter slowly made their way to the gates of the sanctuary where the devoted father gave his favorite daughter to be the bride of our Lord. Silently and slowly the iron gates opened. St. Thérèse stepped in and the gates were closed behind her forever. She was now a Carmelite novice.

### 4. A CARMELITE FOREVER

The months passed quickly and St. Thérèse again stood before the altar and made the promises that bound her for life. As she worked, fasted, and prayed behind the walls of Carmel, she had one great desire. She wished to love our Lord as He had never been loved before. Her love for God was pure because she loved Him for Himself. She often said that she loved Him too much to think of a reward.

"My Jesus," she exclaimed, "You know that I do not serve You for the sake of reward, but only out of love — out of a desire to win souls for You."

Her whole thought was to bring Him joy and happiness. She urged her Sister companions never to let slip the smallest chance of giving joy to God.

Her acts of penance, her prayers, her tasks were performed without any show. The harder and more unpleasant the task, the better she liked it. Never did she consider herself better than the others. In her life she wished nothing unusual to happen. It was her desire that her way to heaven be "the little way" that many others could follow.

All through her life, she showed that little way. It was to live with the trust of a child and to love with the heart of a child. This is what our Lord Himself meant when He said: "Unless you become as little children, you cannot enter the kingdom of heaven."

## 5. Called to Heaven

For a little over nine years, St. Thérèse lived at the Carmel convent. During those years, she cast herself into the arms of God and left herself entirely to Him. When she was only twenty-four years old, God sent her a warning that He would soon take her from this sinful world. Bit by bit, she grew weaker and weaker. However, she insisted on doing her work until close to the very end.

Lying patiently on her bed of pain, she awaited the call of God Whom she had loved and served so well. When all strength had gone from her and severe pains afflicted her, she still smiled because she loved. Some time before she died, she gave a wonderful example of her trust in God by the promises she made. "After my death," she said, "I shall let fall a shower of roses." On another occasion, she remarked, "I shall spend my heaven in doing good upon earth." She relied upon God to make these promises true.

Finally, after much suffering, her last day upon earth came. It was September 30, 1897. She could scarcely breathe.

"The air of earth is failing me," she murmured. "When shall I breathe the air of Heaven?"

Soon she raised herself in bed. The stare of death was in her eyes. "Oh, Mother," she cried, "the chalice of suffering is full to overflowing. My God, do with me as you will, but have pity on me! Sweet Virgin Mother, help me!"

The Sisters were called to her bedside and knelt to recite the prayers for the dying. The dying saint tightly clasped her crucifix in her hands and thanked the Sisters with a smile. With each effort, breathing became more difficult.

She turned to her Mother Superior and whispered, "Mother, am I not going to die?"

The kind Superior gently wiped the brow of her little friend and softly said, "Yes, Sister, you are dying, but you may have to suffer for some time yet."

"Very well, then; be it so!" answered the Little Flower. "I do not wish to suffer less." She gazed at her crucifix and murmured in short broken gasps: "Oh, I love Him! — my God — I — love — You." Her voice died away. She turned her head and was no more.

St. Thérèse lived and died in the quiet little French town of Lisieux. The world had scarcely ever heard its name nor the name of the Carmel convent where the holy nuns offered their prayers and their lives to God. But the Little Flower had been dead only a few years when the whole world sang her praises and when thousands and thousands visited the place made holy by her life. Indeed, since her death she has kept her word by sending showers of roses upon the world — roses of God's favors and blessings.

### QUESTIONS

1. Why was St. Thérèse nervous when she appeared before the pope?
2. How does a Carmelite nun live?
3. Was the father of the Little Flower willing to let her enter the convent?
4. Why did the Superior and the bishop at first refuse to permit her to enter the convent?
5. Why was not the Sisters' habit given to St. Thérèse when she first entered the convent?
6. What one great desire had the Little Flower?
7. What is meant by her "little way"?